What People Are Saying About

Portals, Patterns, and Pathways

A Handbook for Rune Magicians, Star Gazers, and Myth Makers

When you meet teachers so full of knowledge, usually they are dead so you can only read their books! I absolutely cannot wait to get my hands on this book. I have benefitted enormously from attending Imelda's Rune Teaching seminars. The wisdom and voice of the Runes are often present in my work and life. Imelda's teachings bring the perfect balance between historical and language knowledge alongside encourage to experience each Rune's essence via direct revelation.
Katharine Lucy Haworth, Shamanic Teacher, Constellations Practitioner, Red Tent Facilitator, www.orangeblossomoldways.com

What we have in Imelda is the gift of a scholar, deeply knowledgeable about Seidr and the Norse myths, who also lives as a forest witch, seeking what which can only be experienced on the land and felt in our bones. There are many books on runes. Where this one differs is that it offers you the chance to form a true relationship with them. Imelda has created several clever frameworks that allow you to explore inside the runes and feel their true 'aliveness'. If you take the time to absorb the message of this book the runes will become a true companion, and a doorway to a sacred conversation that could change your life.
Trevor Silvester, Training Director of The Quest Institute, founder of Cognitive Hypnotherapy, and author of *Wordweaving: The Science of Suggestion*

Finally – after having organised over 20 webinars with Imelda Almqvist with hundreds of attendees on the mysteries of the Elder Futhark and the old Anglo-Saxon rune row – here it is: Imelda's comprehensive summary of years of research, teaching and working with the runes. Grounded in the historical source material, connecting mythology, astrology, astronomy and Shamanic practices, Imelda hands over the keys to the liminal spaces between the runes. The reader is invited to step through these ancient portals and discover a world connected by the Threads of Fate. This book teaches all you need to know about working with the runes of the Elder Futhark. Fantastic guidance for learning to wield this powerful ancient tool!
Christian Thurow, ShamanPortal Wisdom Webinar coordinator and organiser of the Surbiton Shamanic Circle events

Imelda Almqvist's book *Portals, Patterns, and Pathways* is a ground-breaking exploration of runes that opens new doors for integrating them into modern spiritual practices. With an alternative approach, Imelda weaves together mythology, astrology, and the interconnected relationships of the runes to expand their potential beyond traditional uses. For rune magicians and workers, this provides opportunity for developing a personal, meaningful relationship with the runes, unlocking their greater potential, and enhancing both modern spiritual practices and everyday life.
John Hijatt, host of the *Gifts of the Wyrd* podcast

As I reflect more deeply, I am struck with immense gratitude, a sense of privilege to be called to this work, and an understanding of responsibility. We are a thousand years away from any living ancestors who could have passed this knowledge down to us. Because of Imelda's calling and generous teachings, and all of our individual unique gifts, we will become the living ancestors to those coming after us. Our time is now so their time can come.

My belief is that this work that we collectively embark on is profound and sacred for more reasons than we may now know.
Marie Jo Howell, USA

Imelda showed me how to connect to the runes (I'd tried reading books & got NOWHERE) – she opened the door for me to walk through to a magickal landscape of rune discovery that ceaselessly gives me new gifts of wisdom, healing & illumination. I am forever grateful.
Rachel Goodwin, author of *Sarah's Little Book of Healing: Channeled Techniques from Ascended Master Sarah*

Portals, Patterns, and Pathways

A Handbook for Rune Magicians, Star Gazers, and Myth Makers

Previous Books by Imelda Almqvist

North Sea Water in my Veins
The Pre-Christian spirituality of the Low Countries
ISBN 978-1-78904-906-0

Medicine of the Imagination
Dwelling in Possibility
ISBN 978-1-78904-432-4

Sacred Art, A Hollow Bone for Spirit
Where Art Meets Shamanism
ISBN 978-1-78904-038-8

Natural Born Shamans: A Spiritual Toolkit for Life
Using shamanism creatively with people of all ages
ISBN 978-1-78535-368-0

Portals, Patterns, and Pathways

A Handbook for Rune Magicians, Star Gazers, and Myth Makers

Imelda Almqvist

London, UK
Washington, DC, USA

CollectiveInk

First published by Moon Books, 2026
Moon Books is an imprint of Collective Ink Ltd.,
Unit 11, Shepperton House, 89 Shepperton Road, London, N1 3DF
office@collectiveinkbooks.com
www.collectiveinkbooks.com
www.moon-books.net

For distributor details and how to order please visit the 'Ordering' section on our website.

ISBN: 978 1 917704 19 9
978 1 917704 20 5 (ebook)
Library of Congress Control Number: 2025935376

A CIP catalogue record for this book is available from the British Library.

Design: Lapiz Digital Services

UK: Printed and bound by CPI Group (UK) Ltd, Croydon, CR0 4YY
US: Printed and bound by Thomson-Shore, 7300 West Joy Road, Dexter, MI 48130

The manufacturer's authorised representative in the EU for product safety is:
eucomply OÜ - Pärnu mnt 139b-14, 11317 Tallinn, Estonia, hello@ eucompliancepartner.com,
www.eucompliancepartner.com

Contents

A school without students is only a dream!
My children and my students remain my greatest teachers.

This book is dedicated to Ulric Almqvist, the husband I met at age 19, who sometimes asks: did you fall in love with me or my country? Both!

Acknowledgements

My children and my students are my greatest teachers.

I thank all the people who have attended rune classes with me and all the rune magicians of the past, present and future. You have all added to our collective well and kept the tradition alive!

About the Author

Imelda is an international teacher of Sacred Art and Seiðr/Old Norse Traditions (the ancestral wisdom teachings of Northern Europe). Her previous non-fiction books were all published by Moon Books. Her most recent book is *North Sea Water in My Veins: The Pre-Christian spirituality of the Low Countries.*

The Green Bear is her series of picture book for children, aged 3-8 years. The stories and vibrant artwork, set in Scandinavia, invite children to explore parallel worlds and to keep their sense of magic alive as they grow up.

Imelda has a Forest School in Sweden, situated on the coast of the Baltic Sea, near rune stones, petroglyphs, stone circles and a famous Iron Age grave mound.

Imelda appeared in a TV program, titled *Ice Age Shaman,* made for the Smithsonian Museum, in the series Mystic Britain, talking about Mesolithic arctic deer shamanism. To receive her writing in your inbox at regular intervals, please subscribe *to Imelda Almqvist's Substack*

Foreword

Valarie Budayr

Imelda Almqvist's *Portals, Patterns and Pathways* is nothing short of groundbreaking. This book forms a profound and richly woven tapestry of wisdom, bringing the runes to life in ways that are both innovative and deeply rooted in ancient traditions. Whether you're a seasoned rune magician or someone just beginning to explore this fascinating world, Imelda's insights will guide you on a path of discovery that is as cosmic as it is personal. What truly sets this book apart is Imelda's rare ability to blend rigorous research with intuitive wisdom. Her work invites us to step through portals into the unknown, trace patterns linking runes with star constellations, and walk pathways brimming with mythological depth. The exploration of the liminal spaces between runes as dynamic mysteries filled with mythology is a revelation. This concept alone opens up entirely new dimensions for understanding the Elder Futhark and its connections with the cosmos. Imelda masterfully unpacks the timeless relationships between runes as cultural DNA, showing how these ancient symbols still pulse with relevance and archetypal truth. From mapping the runes as a wheel akin to astrological natal charts to uncovering their relationships as clusters, triads, and opposites, her work redefines how we can connect with the wisdom of the runes. Her insights into how runes reflect ancestral deities and embody universal archetypes provide fertile ground for meditation, study, and practice. The sheer depth of Imelda's scholarship is remarkable. Her dedication to incorporating original Old Norse material, her studies in languages, and her knowledge of mythology across cultures reveal her passion and commitment. Yet, despite this scholarly framework, her writing is welcoming, accessible, and rich in the kind of warmth and humanity that inspires true learning. Perhaps most importantly, this book reminds us that rune work isn't just about decoding ancient symbols; it's about engaging with a living, breathing web of relationships that connect us to the universe, to the divine, and to each other. Imelda's teachings encourage us to honor the sacred, and to recognize the wisdom waiting in wild spaces and mythic realms. This book stands as an invaluable resource for rune enthusiasts, mythology lovers, and those who seek to deepen their spiritual practice. Imelda Almqvist has gifted us with a treasure trove of knowledge, and her work is sure to leave a lasting impact on all who encounter it. Her dedication, vision, and relentless curiosity shine on every page, making this a must-read for anyone called to explore the runes and their timeless mysteries.

Valarie Budayr
www.mongata.org

Preface

Then I started to thrive in fertile space [pollinate]
And I became wise
I grew and so did my wellbeing
A word led to more words
Words led to a deed
Deeds led to more [greater] deeds

Odin's words in Hávamál St.141[1] (My own translation)

Any author knows that words seek the company of words, deeds lead to further deeds and deeds also look for expression through words, to paraphrase the stanza above.

Every liminal space between runes is a mystery school, and its curriculum is mythology.

That insight marked the conception of this book. The runes map a mythical or imaginal realm where cosmic blueprints share their stories and wisdom through archetypal figures, deities, personifications, alchemical images and symbols. We even see glimpses of ancient or forgotten gods.

The Greek philosopher Plato gave us the foundational *Theory of Forms (or Ideas).* He concluded that our physical (or material) world is not as real or true as "Forms". By this he means the non-physical, timeless, absolute, and unchangeable essences of all things, of which objects and matter in the physical world are *merely imitations, or pale reflections.*[2]

In our own time the French philologist and medievalist Claude Lecouteux refers to older ancestral concepts as *resilient structures and enduring ideas.* I think of those patterns of knowledge as "cultural strands of DNA".[3]

All runes are in relationship with all other runes. What happens if I arrange the Runes of the Elder Futhark in a Circle and then look at that circle the way an astrologer reads a natal (birth) chart? Surprising correspondences appear! I am not an astrologer! I can read a natal chart on a basic level, and I also understand the language of symbolism. The method that I present in this book uses only elementary concepts from astrology but no advanced techniques.

The material presented in this book has been test-driven by me and my rune magician students for a period of about nine years.

The Elder Futhark

This book focusses on the runes of the Elder Futhark. Runes are letters of an old Germanic script. Alphabet isn't the right word, because the runes of the Elder Futhark appear in a unique and meaningful sequence (not ABC), which this book explores. There was an Old English word *"run"*, but our word *rune* in English comes from the work of (later) Scandinavian scholars.[4]

Many scripts and alphabets also have a magical dimension. In early cultures speech and writing were often perceived as intrinsically magical acts, linked to Creation itself. Just think of the opening words of the Gospel of St. John in the Bible: "In the beginning was the Word, and the Word was with God, and the Word was God". Now read Odin's words again.

Today we also refer to small stones, bones or antler pieces with these letters carved (or painted) on them as *runes*, or a set of runes. The Elder Futhark consists of 24 characters. Over time it developed into several variations: the Younger Futhark (16 letters), the Anglo-Saxon futhorc (31 letters), the short-twig variations, Medieval Runes and cryptic runes. The Anglo-Saxon Futhorc coexisted with the Northumbrian Runes and the Frisian runes.[5] The Dalecarlian Runes are a late version. Remarkably they remained in use in the isolated Swedish province called Dalarna, well into the 20th century.

Hoarding

This book started life as two separate books because I am a hoarder of esoteric information! The information was compressed into one book. (Key information that was edited out will be published in essays on Substack.) My vision is for this book to be used by rune magicians, looking to access additional dimensions of meaning (from the realms of mythology, cultural astronomy, etymology, folklore etc.) to enrich their rune readings and rune workings.

Popular Misconceptions About the Runes

There was a language spoken in Scandinavia even before Old Norse, we call it Proto-Norse, so Old Norse was the modern language of its own period. The Elder Futhark is not well-suited to writing Old Norse (the vowel sounds don't match up).

The *Poetic Edda* and *Prose Edda* were never written in runes. Nor do we have long texts written or carved in runes (the longest one we have is the inscription on the Rök Rune Stone[6] in Sweden). Some of the text appears in cipher runes and poses a mystery.

The Roman alphabet was introduced in Scandinavia along with Christianity. The *Poetic Edda* and *Prose Edda,* sagas and other long texts were written in the Roman alphabet (and in ink). However, people continued using the runes for carving in stone and writing on leather or bark etc. (following a long ancestral tradition).

A common misunderstanding is that runes were symbols rather than letters. This is not true, they were *primarily used as letters*. In other words: they represented sounds and spoken language.

The Vikings did *not* use the runes of the Elder Futhark (which belong to an earlier period) and Old Norse was *not* written in this script. They used the runes of Younger Futhark.

It is often claimed that the Christian Church actively suppressed the use of runes. The Church certainly introduced Latin, writing in ink and the Roman alphabet but there is no evidence that they actively tried to *eradicate the use of runes* (but they definitely used rune stones as building blocks, we see many rune stones cemented into walls of old churches in Sweden).

One startling feature of rune stones (memorial stones) in Sweden is the large number featuring strikingly Christian motifs (such as crosses and inscriptions, along the lines of "God help Ulfr's soul"). We also find the names of Old Norse Gods in runic inscriptions (e.g. *Thor vigi* – May Thor bless, c. 1000 CE), sometimes on the same stones! There was a transitional period where Old Norse and Christian concepts coexisted. On field trips my students are often baffled by this!

The Vikings were (probably) not covered in runic tattoos. There is not much support for the idea that they had tattoos at all, let alone that they sported the complex fancy bind runes and symbols we see on people today. Only one source, the author Ahmad Ibn Fadlan, mentions dark green "tattoos", but apparently the same word, in Arabic, can also mean (body) paint. The idea (of abundant tattoos) is supported by neither the *Poetic Edda,* the sagas, nor by archaeological findings.[7]

Nearly a millennium divides our era from (the end of) The Viking Age. The Vikings are so popular (and alive in our imagination) right now that many people project their own fantasies onto them and also onto the past. That is understandable and (arguably) empowering, as long we realise that this is the realm of make-believe, not historical accuracy.

A Brief Note About Spelling and Words from Foreign Languages

My research for this book involved dipping into about 25 foreign languages, with six dead ones among them. For a while our family ate dinner with printouts of the Phoenician alphabet, Egyptian hieroglyphs and Hebrew letters on the kitchen table!

I have used the source spelling of foreign language words, unless a common Anglicisation exists. Therefore, Odin rather the Old Norse spelling *Óðinn*.

I have made a distinction between Old Norse and modern Icelandic spelling (and pronunciation). However, not all foreign words have common Anglicised equivalents, so you will encounter (unfamiliar) Nordic letters, such as ö, ǫ, ø, á, å, ð, æ and Þ.

Where I have dipped into alphabets other than the Roman alphabet (used to write modern Western languages) I have provided a transliteration (meaning that I have used the letters which most closely correspond to letters English uses). Example: береза in Russian becomes *bereza* (birch tree).

I have used the Scandinavian names of the runes and spelled them consistently in capital letters (so the reader can easily find them in the text when looking up a reference). Anglo-Saxon variants of those names are provided only once, in Chapter 1. Therefore: *BJARKA (Berkana or Berkano) – the Birch Rune.*

Where I have quoted other authors or texts, I have used their preferred spelling for Old Norse words. I have used the Sanskrit word "karma" throughout, instead of the Old Norse word "ørlǫg", to facilitate ease of comprehension.

I personally use the Uthark sequence, not the standard sequence of the Elder Futhark and I explain why in Chapter 1. In the text I also point out where and why this order makes more sense to me. Having said that, every reader is invited to arrive at their own conclusion and use the wheel of the runes as a dial, accessing all possibilities and significations. Please use the Futhark sequence if that feels right to you.

Abbreviations Used:

ON = Old Norse
OE = Old English
SW = Contemporary Swedish
AS = Anglo-Saxon
(*) – The asterisk indicates a Proto-Germanic reconstruction (meaning that this form is so ancient that we have no record of it, but linguists have deduced this from later recorded languages, with much detective work and observing the rules governing the way languages evolve. Those linguists work backwards from contemporary English, Dutch and Danish etc.)

Part I

Chapter 1

Sacred Cows: Futhark or Uthark?

Let's introduce the runes!

This book is about working with the runes of the Elder Futhark. I have created two illustrations for this chapter. The first one shows the runes organised in the standard Futhark Sequence, with both their Scandinavian and Anglo-Saxon Names. The second illustration shows the runes organised in the Uthark Sequence (and I have also provided the core meanings of the runes, to make it a handy reference list).

The Futhark Sequence

1 FE FEHU	2 UR URUZ	3 THURS THURISAZ	4 ASS ANSUZ
5 REID RAIDHO	6 KEN KENAZ	7 GIFU GEBO	8 WYNJA WUNJO
9 HAGAL HAGALAZ	10 NAUD NAUTHIZ	11 IS ISA	12 JARA JERA
13 PERTHRA PERTHRO	14 EOH EIWAZ	15 ALGIZ	16 SOL SOWILO
17 TYR TIWAZ	18 BJARKA BERKANA	19 EH EHWAZ	20 MADR MANNAZ
21 LAGU LAGUZ	22 ING INGUZ	23 ODAL OTHALA	24 DAGAZ

Including Anglo-Saxon Names

The Futhark Sequence

(including the Anglo-Saxon rune names)

The Uthark Sequence

1 UR aurochs	2 THURS Thor, giant	3 ASS God (Odin)	4 REID riding, wheel journey
5 KEN pine torch	6 GIFU gift, exchange hieros gamos	7 WYNJA joy	8 HAGAL hail, crisis
9 NAUD need, necessity restriction	10 IS ice	11 JARA harvest year	12 PERTHRA rock (cave)
13 EOH yew axis mundi	14 ALGIZ elk, moose protection	15 SOL sun	16 TYR spiritual warrior
17 BJARKA birch (mother)	18 EH horse, death twins, partners	19 MADR mankind (ancestors)	20 LAGU water
21 ING seed	22 ODAL homestead	23 DAGAZ light illumination	24 FE cattle wealth

Including the core meanings

The Uthark Sequence

(including the core meanings of all runes)

The Uthark Theory

There is a theory (disputed and controversial but underpinned by some compelling arguments) that in a time of great upheaval, after Scandinavia converted to Christianity, rune magicians and teachers of esoteric (controversial, risky) material were forced to preserve powerful material by using ciphers (a code for encryption). After all, witch hunts happened in Scandinavia too.

Rune Weel as a "Dial"

In classes I often use the metaphor of a dial. A dial can be turned clockwise or anticlockwise to activate a new setting or program (just think of your washing machine). One theory proposes that rune magicians deliberately dialled the wheel of the runes back by one position, meaning that the last rune (FE/Feoh/Fehu) became the first rune. Let's examine the meanings of the runes involved:

Following the mainstream system, Futhark rune #1 FE refers to mobile wealth in the form of cattle, meaning *domesticated cows*. Wealth used to be expressed as the number of cattle a person owned. FE refers to material wealth and is etymologically related to the modern word "fee".

In contrast Rune #2 UR (URUZ) refers to a great reservoir of untamed energies (or potential) which have not yet divided, polarised or taken any definite form or focus. We can engage and dance with these forces – but we cannot control or direct them. They are primordial and feral.

I view UR as the rune of Audhumbla, (the primordial cow was in the company of giant Ymir). I believe that the sequence of the runes tells the story of creation and, by extension, the story of all cycles, great and small. It seems unlikely that domesticated cattle, or indeed any concept of money, existed at the very beginning of the cosmic cycle we currently find ourselves in. Domesticated cattle and wealth first occur in the Neolithic period, in Europe. Before then, the hunter-gathering tribes could not accumulate wealth, because they had to carry all their possessions with them. That is why I believe that the circle of the runes opens with UR (the feral aurochs) and closes with FE (tamed animals, cattle).

Some rune magicians accept the Uthark Theory and others reject it. Working with the Uthark brings profound correspondences and wisdom teachings. But equally powerful correspondences are found with the dial set to Futhark. I tell all my students to *try both.*

We don't know who arranged the runes of the Elder Futhark in a particular order or exactly when this occurred. We do not know either why it does not follow the phonetic letter order of nearly all European alphabets. What we do know is that the order of the runes in the Elder Futhark is based on ancient rune stones.

The *Kylver Stone* on the Swedish island of Gotland, dating from about 400 CE, is known for listing each of the runes of the Elder Futhark in a specific order, with the runes representing A (ASS), S (SOL) and B (BJARKA) mirrored compared to later convention. ALGIZ appears upside down. The F (FE) and W (WYNJA) runes are only partially inscribed. This gives us:

Inscription on the Kylver Stone

This sequence still poses some mysteries. It is not completely clear that the first rune is FE. The final rune is an odd rune too (resembling a tree) with six twigs on the left side and eight on the right side of a single stave. This could be a cipher rune, but we do not know for sure.

The field of numerology (as well as the study of ancient scripts and alphabets) tells us that the position of every letter or number has unique connotations, related to cosmology (and, as we will see later, archaeo-astronomy).

A German psychotherapist called Bert Hellinger pioneered Family Constellations work, a therapeutic approach focussed on revealing hidden dynamics within families of relationships. In this work a constellation (or grouping, a physical set-up) is created. Then neutral people (who are not enmeshed or emotionally invested in the original family or situation) take up key positions in that grouping and report what they experience there (a sense of restriction or freedom, strong emotions, flashes of insight etc).[1]

What I learned from this field is that once a symbol is placed in a numbered slot, it assumes the attributes of that position. In plain English: *positioning and sequence matter.* Just like psychologists have demonstrated that your position in the birth order and family matter, and impacts your life. Therefore, the position that we allocate to runes is important. *(However, any connection between runes and numerology was only made by rune magicians long after the Viking Age, in the 17th century.)*[2]

The runes are portals or cosmic gateways. They continue to reveal new dimensions of meaning all the time. I do not believe that one single person can ever know all there is to know about the runes. They reveal as much as any apprentice or rune magician is ready to absorb at a given time. They also reflect the times we live in and yield new meanings as world history scrolls through larger ages. The runes will meet us wherever we are, whoever we are.

Astrologically speaking we are making a collective shift from the Age of Pisces into the Age of Aquarius, and groups of people appear to be working out collective karma, in different locations on the time-space continuum. (I define karma as unfinished business, not divine punishment). One helpful concept from astrology is that the outer planets (Jupiter, Saturn, Uranus, and Neptune) show *generational influences* in natal charts. Because they are so far away, they appear to move through our chart more slowly (I am referring to their speed *as perceived from Earth*) than the inner planets (Mercury, Venus, Earth, and Mars).

Entire generations share the same placements, indicating that these groups of people are working through similar themes at the same time. Then a paradigm shift occurs, and a new generation faces a completely new set of themes and challenges. This shift generally overturns the values and limits of the previous generation, which causes stress, especially between parents and children (but less so between children and their grandparents). I find these principles helpful both in my shamanic work with young people and in rune magician work.[3]

Examples of such themes in our day are a (relatively new) internet-driven world with AI now changing the world again, only a few decades later. Ours is a world of short attention spans, constant dopamine hits, a significant reduction in time spent physically with peers and an astounding rise in diagnoses of Autistic Spectrum Disorders and ADD.

Another theme is gender dysphoria and the claims of oppression, fragility and a demand for safe spaces. There is also a public focus on decolonisation (of both countries and individual mindsets). In its wake came a remarkable shift away from scientific evidence-based thinking (in transgender and intersectional ideology).

Basic facts in biology have been overturned (people are born "in the wrong body" and gender is "assigned at birth" as opposed to being an observable biological fact). Our culture currently accepts that gender can be announced and changed by a process of self-identification, meaning that I could declare myself a man tomorrow, if I so wished. Even 1 + 1 is no longer 2 (because maths, punctuality and rationality are *colonial* or *racist* values). We see a veritable *smörgåsbord* for generational astrologers and social commentators here!

The Norns Carving Ørlǫg

The Old Norse word for karma is *ørlǫg*. It means primal law (literally "what has been carved") and it refers to everything that informs or shapes our current reality. Everything that came before (actions, deeds, thoughts, inventions, key decisions) has set certain *trains in motion*. Many such patterns (or imprints) are ancestral and ancient, dating back to the time of our Deep Ancestors. Evolutionary psychologists point out that distress is caused by the fact that we humans have an existence completely out of synch with the hunter-gathering lifestyle our bodies and minds were designed (or evolved) for.

We can learn a lot from studying the names of the Norns (the powers of fate, represented by three women). Urd or Urðr (ON, over time her name becomes the word Wyrd in old English and eventually Weird in modern English) refers to the very beginning or source of something, something primal or primordial. Her name is often translated as *the past*, but more correctly it refers to *past events still working themselves out in the present time*. Time is a great mystery. We only ever inhabit the "Now". I see an undeniable connection between Rune UR and Urd.

The next Norn is called Verdandi (ON *Verðandi)*. Her name is derived from the Old Norse verb for "being": it refers to *what is continually coming into being*. Her name is usually translated as *the present*, but "always becoming" is a more precise translation.

The third Norn is Skuld. People call her *the future*, but that is way off the mark. Her name means *debt*. Her name refers to that "what is being owed" (meaning what is unresolved, imbalanced or not in harmony) and needs to be worked out in the present time. In plain English that takes the form of ancestral pain and debt, intercultural (geopolitical) tension and inequalities, and our own personal issues needing to be worked on in *the here and now.*

Their names teach us that the past is not a closed book and that the future does not exist, as it is not a given or a promise (and we never truly inhabit it). Ragnarok (personal or collective destruction) always looms, in the Old Norse perspective. We are not entitled to a future. What does exist is the spiritual obligation to pay our personal and ancestral debts: to heal our lives, do shadow work and ancestral healing work. To uphold human rights and do cross-cultural healing work. You could say that this is how we repay the Gift (GIFU) of Life.

The runes are not only letters (or glyphs), they also have powerful in-dwelling spirits. The runes may well represent deities and point to lost deities and myths.

Frisian Runes, Blank Runes, and Reversed Runes

I work primarily with the runes of the Elder Futhark. As a Dutch rune magician, I also work with the Frisian Rune Row because it reflects my ancestry most closely. I spoke the West Frisian dialect in childhood.[4]

Students often ask me about working with reversed runes or a blank rune. I do not use a blank rune because the 24 runes of the Elder Futhark are eloquent enough to convey anything (even: *stop asking questions!)*

I don't work with reversed runes either, because every rune has both a light side and shadow side, as does every human being and every phenomenon known on Earth. Let me emphasize that I am not speaking of good and evil here. The light side refers to the life-giving processes of creation unfolding, beginnings and growth, while the dark side refers to death, dismantling and endings (in every possible manifestation).

They are flip sides of the same coin: creation cannot exist without destruction. Destruction clears space for new beginnings. The very building blocks for creation are freed up by the processes of death, dismemberment and decomposition. Symbolic death is a force to be reckoned with too. The runes will eloquently express how those forces play out in human lives and world events. The runes will still speak to the grandchildren of our grandchildren, who will inhabit a world we cannot even imagine right now. The runes will remain a powerful tool.

Every single rune can pose the starting point for a journey around the wheel. Life and learning are cyclical, not linear, processes.

Chapter 2

The Runes Unadorned

Some Basics

The modern word *rune* comes to us from the Proto-Germanic (reconstructed) stem *runo, via Old Norse (*run* meant secret, magic sign or runic character) and Old English (mystery, mysterious statement or secret council). In Old High German *runa* meant a secret conversation or whisper.

The magical work with runes largely ended in the mid-15th century, when the first witch trials were held. For two centuries a Dark Age occurred in formal rune studies, but in the late 17th century German philologists reintroduced the word in their writings. Rune magicians started rediscovering (and re-constructing) a lot of material from the 17th century onward.

However, from a rural or grassroots point of view *the runes never disappeared and they were never re-discovered.* They have always been used in the folk traditions and in *trolldom* (SW, folk magic). Christianisation certainly affected that and restricted the use of runes– but never fully eradicated that.

The runes were letters but they were also used in magical workings, at least by some groups in society, some of the time. Before literacy became the norm in Western society, all forms of writing had an aura of mystery and secrecy. The Roman Catholic Church uses Latin until today. Just think of the impact on the human senses of Latin mixed with frankincense!

Students often ask why all rune rows are angular. This is not completely true, later Medieval Runes are curved, and dots were used as diacritical signs (changing the pronunciation of a letter). However, the first runes were carved primarily on hard material which offers resistance (wood, bone, antler, metal etc.) and it is much easier to cut straight lines than curvy ones.

The Old English names of all 24 runes of the Elder Futhark, along with five names unique to the Anglo-Saxon runes, are preserved in the Old English rune poem (dating from the 7th century).[1]

The Norse names of the Elder Futhark were reconstructed, working back in time, based on three rune poems we have been left: the Old Norwegian Rune Poem, the Old Icelandic Rune Poem and the Old English Rune Poem. This means that those names were all puzzled out *later* by scholars. We have not been left an operating manual.

My students often ask about a possible connection between petroglyphs in Scandinavia (carved about 2,700 years ago) and the runes of the Elder Futhark (used from the 2nd to the 8th century). The short answer is that we don't know, we have no evidence for this, but some petroglyphs resemble runes.

In our day people schooled in esoteric disciplines, or folk magic, write books and make YouTube videos. This material has never been more accessible – and that brings a shadow: in the wrong hands it can be used to do harm. This is a significant downside of the democratization of occult knowledge. A little knowledge can be a very dangerous thing indeed; and not knowing how little you know is even more dangerous!

Different theories exist about the origin of the runes. They are easily found online. My own research explores a connection between the order of early alphabets and the Zodiac. *Archeoastronomy* is the field that studies the night sky, as it was perceived by early astronomers. One question I attempt to answer in this book is how the runes, and the order in which the runes appear, relate to old star patterns and constellations.

The Uthark Sequence

With Core Meanings

***URUZ/UR** – *U or OO*

Wild and untamed energies, a void teeming with potentialities, "back to the drawing board".

Mostly likely relates to the aurochs, an extinct species of large wild cattle. Their horns were used as drinking vessels by Vikings. Germanic youths tested their skill and strength against these animals (think of bull fights in Spain).

***THURISAZ/THURS** – *TH (Þ, þ)*

Rune of Thor and the Giants (forces of chaos). In Anglo-Saxon England: thorn.

Early scholars rediscovering the Norse material translated certain beings in Norse Cosmology as *giants*. This is a misnomer. They are an earlier race or tribe of beings than the Norse gods. They possess immense knowledge and superpowers, but they are not (generally) oversized in the way that our word giant implies. Some people now use the ON word Jǫtunn instead. They intermarry with Norse gods and produce semi-divine offspring. The Norns are described as "giant maidens" in the Vǫluspá.

***ANSUZ/ASS or OSS** – *A or AH*

Rune of Odin, god rune, divine speech (breath) and ecstatic work. The plural of ASS is Aesir (gods).

The OE rune poem replaces ASS with OS (mouth), which may refer to Odin's qualities of eloquence, divine speech, poetic frenzy, and prophecy.

***RAIÐO/RAD/REIÐ** – *R*

Riding, rune related to motion and wheels, the wagons of the gods. By extension: circles and cycles, time, stories, music and rhythm.

***KAUNAZ/*KENAZ/ CEN/ KAUN – K**

(Pine) torch. By extension: creativity, metallurgy, blacksmith and forge.

OE *cen* means firebrand while the ON *kaun* means ulcer.

***GEBO/GYFU/GIFU – G**

Gift, the act of giving, making a sacrifice to the gods, sacred reciprocity: "A gift in return for a gift" (Hávamál).

The exchange of gifts and favours creates deep and lasting bonds between human beings. Our paths cross and so do our *ørlǫgþátto* (threads of fate).

***WUNJO/WEN/WYNJA** – *W*

Frigg's rune of joy, pleasure, harmony and connotations of affectionate relationships (OE *wine* is friend, the contemporary Swedish word for friend is *vän*).

***HAGALAZ/HAEGL/HAGAL** – *H*

Hail, sudden cataclysmic change and rune of witches.

***NAUÐIZ/NYD/NAUD** – *N*

Need, distress, necessity, ordeals, adversity and restriction.

***IS/IS (OE)/IS – I** *(EE in phonetic English).*

Literally ice. Time on ice, being becalmed, reflection and clarity.

***JERA/ GER/AR/JARA** – *J/Y*

Year and harvest. Rune of agriculture, seasons and the cycles of fertility.

***EIHWAZ/ EOH/EOH** – *"EI" (a diphthong in Dutch and German).*

Yew tree. *iw* or *eow* in Old English. Axis mundi, spine, rotational axis.

***PERTH/PEORTH/PERTHRA** – *P*
Dice cup. The rune of rocks, caves and mountains (in Scandinavia).

***ALGIZ/EOHLSEDG/YR** – *Z (not A)*
The key meaning is protection. Animal powers. Possible connection to the Germanic divine twins, the Alcis, cited by Tacitus. In the Younger Futhark this rune turns upside down.

***SOWULO/SIGEL/SOL** – *S*
The sun was perceived as a female "giantess" in Norse cosmology; perceived as travelling in a ship on her journey across the sky, in Bronze Age petroglyphs. In the Eddas she is the sister of Máni (the male Moon) and pulled across the Heavens by two horses (in her chariot). Both Sun and Moon are pursued by wolves.

***TEIWAZ/TIR/TYR** – *T*
Spiritual warrior, sacrifice for a greater good, justice.
Some scholars believe that Tyr was an earlier principal Germanic god, before Odin took over. His rune is an arrow. Arrows also appear in many Bronze Age rock carvings.

***BERKANA/BEORC/BJARKAN** – *B*
Birch tree.
In Slavic cosmology there is a strong association with motherhood, fertility and rites of passage for young women.

***EHWAZ/EOH/EH** – *E (AY in phonetic English)*
The Horse Rune, also of twins, partnership, traveling between the worlds and death.
German tribes used horses for divination and sacrifice.

***MANNAZ/MANN/MADR** – *M*

The rune of mankind, (all human beings), including our ancestors and descendants. Tacitus wrote that Mannus was the son of Tuisto and the progenitor of the three Germanic tribes: the *Ingaevones, Herminones and Istvaeones.*[2]

****LAGUZ/LOGR/LAGU** – L*

Water in all its manifestations: river, sea, lake, blood and bodily fluids etc.

In Jutland (Denmark) slaves were sacrificed by drowning, in the Nerthus cult.

***INGUZ/INGWAZ/ING** – *NG*

Seed, fertility, storehouse of potential life force.

As Yngvi this rune is connected to Norse god Freyr: fertility and virility.

OTHALA/EDEL/ODAL – *OH or OO (in phonetic English).*

Homeland, homestead, enclosed space, family home or ancestral home.

***DAGAZ/DAEG/DAGAZ** – *D*

Day or daylight, symbolically: enlightenment, illumination, higher perspective.

***FEHU/ FEOH/FE** – *F*

Cattle, mobile wealth, money (our contemporary word *fee* is etymologically related).

The wagon of ancient goddess Nerthus was drawn by cows and India still reveres sacred cows.

Note: Odal often appears as the last rune of the Common Germanic runes. There is an alternative sequence where two swaps occur: ODAL and DAGAZ swap places and so do PERTRHA and EOH.

Chapter 3

Getting to Know the Runes

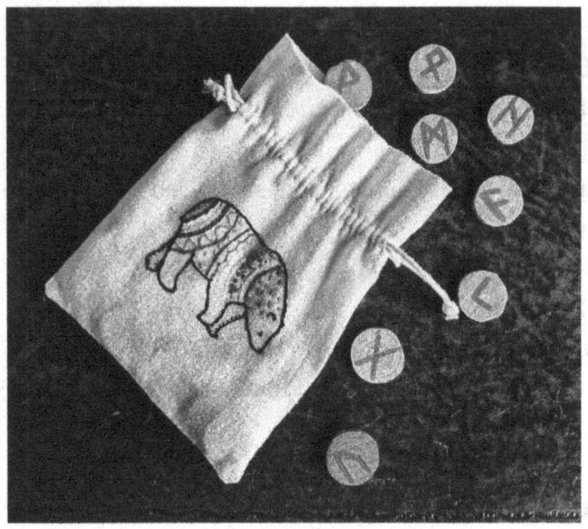

Rune Pouch

This chapter provides the (basic) guidance I give all my rune magician students.

Learning the runes takes time and focus. You can buy rune sets but I strongly recommend that you make your own (popular options are: wood chips, pebbles or antler slices). Carefully consider the kind of wood (and any magical or esoteric associations). My own runes are made from the branch of a juniper struck by lightning.

Most people work with the runes of the Elder Futhark. Explore all options and decide on the names you will use: the Ango-Saxon names or the Nordic ones? Will you follow the Futhark or Uthark sequence? (I suggest that you try all options before you commit).

Once You Have Your Set of Runes

- Make (or a find) a dedicated pouch to keep them in (a drawstring is handy for pulling runes).
- Make your own personal information sheet about the runes, using the names and sequence of your choice.
- Chant the names of all runes daily (that will cement the names and order in your memory).
- Pick one rune every morning and use it to read (predict) the energy signature of the day ahead.
- Also pick a rune every evening and reflect on how that rune mirrors key events or dynamics of your day.
- Dream with the runes: put a different rune under your pillow every night and keep a dream journal about runes.
- Go for walks and look for runes all around you: in twigs on the pavement, markings on roads, flights paths of birds (e.g. KEN and the V formation of geese.) and so forth.

Many people do not move beyond learning the names and meanings of individual runes (most commonly the Elder Futhark) and doing rune readings for themselves and others. That is fine because the runes can be a tremendous help in everyday life, gaining clarity and making decisions. However, from teaching my own students I know that once people master this stage of learning, there is often a yearning for going deeper, reading more complex patterns and accessing more layers of wisdom.

The Next Level

Start pulling runes for yourself on specific questions. Avoid questions which invite a yes or no answer. Instead ask for the runes to provide *guidance or insight* on an issue or situation.

Once you gain confidence, offer some rune readings to friends or family. Explain that you are a beginner looking for guinea pigs (reduce stress by reducing expectations!)

Make yourself a *cheat sheet*: draw the runes and some key words for their meanings. Keep that sheet at hand.

Every rune reading for another person will teach you something significant and expand your understanding of the runes. Keep a rune magician journal.

More Advanced Level

Start making bindrunes and sigils.

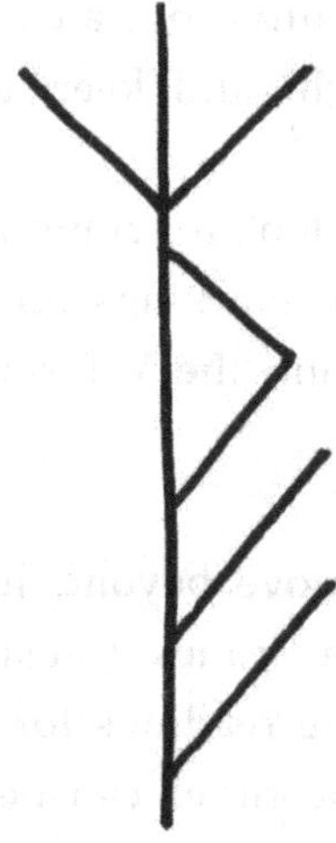

A bindrune

Meditate on the bindrune in the picture. Which runes does it consist of? What might be the meaning this bindrune conveys and condenses?

A sigil is a design or picture that packs power and contains magic. Sigils can be made from runes. Here is the most basic form, a sigil of my first name. I used rune HAGAL in its form of a six-pointed star, with the six letters of my name on the ends:

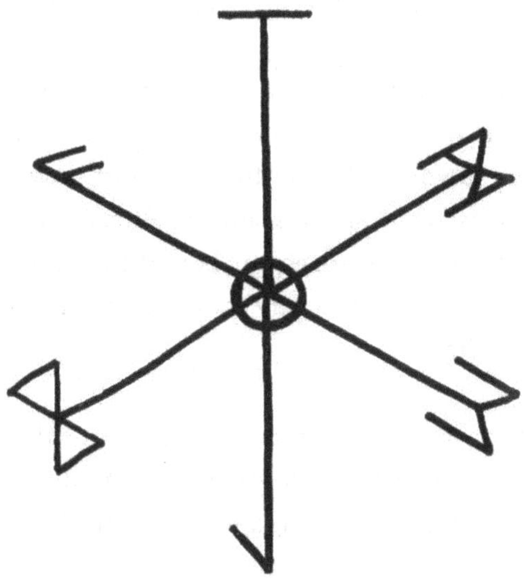

Basic First Name Sigil

If your name has less than six letters: choose additional runes that have meaning for you or reflect a quality you possess (e.g. TYR: spiritual warrior).

If your name has more than six letters: use bindrunes (or make a sigil with more spokes).

Of course, you can also make a sigil for your surname, or combining both names.

If you are in love, you can the combine the name of you and "your person" etc.

Sigils can also be made from other symbols or glyphs. You can be eclectic and combine characters from different traditions or origins, (as long as they have meaning for you). Get as creative as you like!

Complex Rune Readings

Do more complex rune readings. For instance, a traditional Norn spread:

> Draw three boxes on a piece of paper. One box is for Urðr (what has already come to pass or the origin of things). The middle box is for Verðandi, (what is currently taking shape). The third box is for Skuld. The future never arrives (we always inhabit "the here and now") but this box shows us what is imbalanced, where are any debts we need to pay? Pull three runes and put them in those boxes. Also interpret the way they interact and follow on from each other.

Consider taking a class in rune magic. Recordings of classes in runes and rune magic are available in my online school (Pregnant Hag Teachings, named for the indwelling spirit of the HAGAL Rune.)

Once you are comfortable doing most of these things, proceed deeper into this book and try some innovative ways of working with the runes.

Chapter 4

Three "Aettir" (Rune Families)

You already know that the runes of the Elder Futhark can be arranged in either the (dominant) Futhark sequence or (more esoteric) Uthark sequence.[1]

Why Aettir?

The Old Norse word *ǽttir* means families. Historians use it when writing about generations of families and kinship, (often people who have the same surname, or lived on the same family farm). The mythologist Georges Dumézil[2] (writing around 1940) formulated a tripartite hypothesis, which divided Indo-European society into three classes:

- Sacred sovereign (Priest/King)
- Warrior
- (Food) producer (Farmer)

Rune magicians borrowed this division and connected to the Aettir (three rune families). Traditionally the runes of the Futhark are divided into three families or groupings of eight runes each. If we follow the dominant order of the runes (The Futhark Sequence) this leads us to three Aettir and all have male leaders:

- First Aett of the Nurturer/Farmer
- Second Aett of the Warrior
- Third Aett of the Sovereign/Priest/King/Ruler

Medieval society had a similar division: *"those who pray, those who labour and those who fight"*.[3]

The Aettir, Using the Futhark Sequence

First Aett: Runes 1 – 8

Second Aett: Runes 9 – 16

Third Aett: Runes 17 – 24

Aett #1 FE – UR – THURS – ASS – REID – KEN – GIFU – WYNJA

The Aett of Freyr

The first family is responsible for fertility and growth cycles on Earth.

Aett #2 HAGAL – NAUD – IS – JARA – PERTHRA – EOH – ALGIZ – SOL

The Aett of Heimdallr

Heimdallr stands on watch by the bridge to Asgard. When Ragnarok starts he will warn everyone by blowing his gjallarhorn. Ragnarok is the ultimate HAGAL event!

The second family deals with the challenges human beings face on Earth: the matters of fate and destiny, ordeals and initiations, loss and grief, (symbolic) death and resurrection.

Aett #3 TYR – BJARKA – EH – MADR – LAGU – ING – ODAL – DAGAZ

Tyr's Aett

The third family opens the astronomical season. It refers to the greater cosmic cycles of Precession and the 'changing of the guards' in terms of pole stars. Tyr is the spiritual warrior and protector of the collective.

The Aettir, Using the Uthark Sequence

Let us now look closely at the Aettir of the Uthark. They all have female leaders and this offers a wonderful complementarity.

Aett #1 UR – THURS – ASS – REID – KEN – GIFU – WYNJA – HAGAL

Aett of UR, Norn Urdr and Audhumbla

The first family open with the creation of our current world (universe) and describes the agricultural year: Mother Earth splitting open and receiving the seeds that human beings plant.

Aett #2 NAUD – IS – JARA – PERTHRA – EOH – ALGIZ – SOL – TYR

Aett of the Norns, the human condition and the Powers of Fate

The second family tells the Hero Journey of all human beings. They face the judgment of the Norns, adversity, opposition and restriction. Rune SOL lights up the cave (the tomb-womb at PERTHRA) and promises a new day and new future.

Aett #3 BJARKA – EH – MADR – LAGU – ING – ODAL – DAGAZ – FE

Bjarka's Aett, Aett of the Cosmic Cycles and Balancing

The third family continues the universal themes of the second aett, but on a larger (cosmic) scale. This takes us into the domain of both astronomy and astrology.

Aettir Defined by their Final Rune

I have probably subjected you to information overload, so you may wish to take a break and digest what came before.

The Aettir can also be defined by their *final runes*. For the Uthark this creates the following line-up:

Aett #1 HAGAL

For Norse rune magicians HAGAL is the rune of witches and witchcraft. This makes Freyja the leader of this Aett. As Gullveig/Heidr she went out in the world and taught Seiðr to women. She is the First Witch!

Aett #2 TYR

Giving Tyr the leading role makes this the Aett where human beings become spiritual warriors.

Aett #3 FE

This is the aett of domesticated cattle and a settled lifestyle (agriculture, large farms). Its figurehead is the cow. She represents the nourishing principle. On a much larger scale this represents (or eventually becomes) civilization as we know it (large cities, theatre and fine art, office jobs, the welfare or "nanny" state etc.) It is also the aett of capitalism, where money rules all major decisions.

The leaders of every Aett switch in a very interesting way when we switch from Futhark to Uthark:

Futhark Sequence

1. Freyr
2. Heimdallr
3. Tyr

Male divinities

Uthark Sequence

1. Urdr/Audhumbla (UR)
2. The Norns (NAUD)
3. Cosmic Mother/Healer/Apothecary (BJARKA)

Female divinities

To work with Aettir, first identify what you wish to accomplish (plant seeds, harvest or dismember a relational script or societal structure?) Do you need courage or an invisibility cloak?

Look for the closest match in terms of leader and family. Invite them to work with you (and/or your client) on certain issues.

Aettir can also be used to identify natural progression. They will, for instance, teach you that creation cannot exist without destruction, and that periods of growth require periods of stagnation and "dwindling".

Use the magical principles of reversing, disrupting or flipping. If your client has problems of a "patriarchal nature", change the dial and put female rune leaders on the case.

Rather than working with one rune at the time, you can now put a family of eight runes on a situation or unresolved matter. They can guide you through complex processes in a way that is ethical and spiritually sound.

The bottom-line is: respect free will and request consent whenever permission is required.

The Gjallarhorn of FE

The Gjallarhorn (literally *yelling horn*) blown by Heimdallr at the start of Ragnarok is probably the horn of a steer or oxen: rune FE.

As the sound of the Gjallarhorn indicates the end of the world, this is another (strong) argument for putting FE in the final (not first) position.

Many traditions teach that in the very beginning there was a sound. In popular language we speak of a Big Bang. Babies cry at birth. The first being is Ymir and his name means *screamer*. Are all those things connected? Does Heimdallr usher in a new world by blowing the Gjallarhorn? Is there a bridge of sound (or vibration) between our universe and the "next" one?

The Wheel of runes keeps on turning. We now plunge back into the cauldron of chaotic yet generative energies of UR and another trip around the wheel unfolds.

Chapter 5

Natural Relationships Between Runes

This chapter focusses on *natural relationships between the runes*. This refers to relationships set by order, sequence and positioning.

Here are some ground rules I formulated over a period of years:

- Every rune is in relationship with every other rune.
- At every rune we already see a foreshadowing of the next rune. (E.g. we see glimpses of both Frigg and Freyja at GIFU, but they appear in their fullness at WYNJA and HAGAL respectively).
- Runes are in a particularly close relationship with the runes flanking them in the rune row sequence and with their "polar opposites" (the runes opposite them on the wheel, I call this phenomenon *polar pairs*).
- Runes also form clusters: triads, tetrads and even larger groups. A very powerful example of this is the GIFU – WYNJA – HAGAL Triad.
- Both *axes* and *triads* can consist of *any* combination of runes.
- We always find all the runes (the entire circle) when we exhaustively map the significations and associations of one single rune (*runes within runes)*.
- Runes can be paired up with other concepts to cast further light on complex situations.
- Those 'other things' can be concepts from the Old Norse Traditions (anatomy of soul, the domains or halls of the gods etc.) or concepts from a completely different field or tradition (the seven Christian virtues or cardinal sins,

Carl G. Jung's archetypes, concepts from astrology or the kabbalah etc.)

- Runes can also form *rune axes* and *triads* with runes from other rune rows (meaning runes we do *not* find in the Elder Futhark).
- All runes point to ancient Norse deities and may well have represented divinities once. Worded differently: *the in-dwelling spirits of the runes are ancient deities.*
- The spaces between the runes are powerful liminal or transitional zones where we find myths, archetypes and wisdom teachings. Those zones have otherworld beings as guardians and inhabitants.

The possibilities are limitless, especially so for people who blend several cosmologies or traditions (something rune magicians have done for centuries).

Runes Within Runes

One helpful task for a novice rune magician is meditating on how runes often appear to contain (or consist of) other runes.

For example: Rune JARA consists of two KEN runes. Do they represent crescents, (perhaps the waxing and waning moon), or perhaps twins Freyr and Freyja, who both have a connection to matters of fertility, harvests and abundance?

Those KEN runes can be broken into smaller segments: two IS runes each. Do we find two ice runes in the rune representing fire in the Elder Futhark? Does this point to the Norse creation story about Fire and Ice?

Beyond visual elements, we also find *runes within runes* when we explore all possible meanings of a rune. Obviously, rune JARA (harvest) contains ING (seed) but dig deeper: humans (MADR) plant the seed, it needs watering (LAGU), the scythe cuts the grain (EH) etc. Ultimately JARA represents the entire growth cycle, meaning it contains the wheel of the runes. *All runes do, if you sit with them long enough!*

Within REID (cosmic cycle) we find the Sun (and the Moon, planets and stars) etc.

A professor of mathematics once told me that between every two numbers, and even between every two fractions, we find *"an infinity of infinities"*. The same thing is true for the runes.

Runic Axes

A runic axis can be visualised as a line drawn between any two runes on the Wheel.

The runes all have unique indwelling spirits. They all have relationships with each other and form complex clusters of meaning and power.

One powerful concept is working with *rune axes*, this being the plural of the word 'axis' (I am not referring to a weapon!) Every rune, in an established rune row (visualised as a circle or wheel), is in relationship with all other runes. In that way the runes form natural pairs and groupings; a *very* large number of them.

I asked my brother, Stephan Berendsen, (a physics teacher) to do the math: 24 runes paired in any possible combination (assuming there is no preference of sequence) gives us 276 options or combinations.

The next level is to work with *runic triads* (groups of three runes), which gives us an even larger field of permutations, mathematically speaking I arrive at: 2,024 combinations.[1]

Once we create even larger groupings: quartets, quintets or even (new) aettir (groups of eight runes) the number of permutations starts rising to infinity.

Everyday situations are messy entangled affairs, a constellation of many different influences (and moving parts). If you and I do not agree on something, it is likely that we see things through different lenses. Your lens might be THURS–TYR *(division, only one of us is right and ultimately victorious!)* and my lens might be BJARKA – LAGU *(there is no definite answer but a solution will appear if we allow the waters of intuition to dissolve the space between extremes).*

Centuries of magical work by rune magicians have created an energetic reservoir of knowledge that we can tap into and *even add to.* You will find a compendium of all rune axes in Part II of this book.

Teamwork: Special Runic Relationships

Runes form close relationships with other runes by virtue of the following principles:

- Every rune has a special relationship with the rune I call its *polar opposite,* meaning the rune that sits exactly 180 degrees across from it on the wheel: they form *polar pairs.*
- *Natural polarities exist within the meanings of the runes* and they form natural pairs too, opening up a wide spectrum of meanings.
- Every rune forms a meaningful triad with the runes it is flanked by: this grouping is PRECEDING RUNE – RUNE – FOLLOWING RUNE.
- Additionally, any rune also forms triads with any other two runes. Often those triads tell an archetypal story or myth, a blueprint of creation.
- In a rune reading, *runic relationships* can tell us a lot about our relationships with ourselves, with key challenges in our life, with other people etc.
- Runes can also form pairs, triads and other couplings with other things (such as plants, trees, concepts psychology or aspects of soul). This is a concept my students and I use in *soul map readings* (see Chapter 10).

Example of Natural Polarity Within a Rune

WYNJA is the rune of joy. In a rune reading with a person suffering from clinical depression it may indicate *a lack of joy, a need for more joy*. You might create an amulet with this rune carved on it, for them to wear on their person.

Some people assign meaning to *reversed runes* (runes pulled in a mirrored, inverted or reversed position). However, some runes always look the same, upright or reversed (for instance the cross that is GIFU). These runes will still contain the full continuum of all possible meanings.

Polar Pairs

One obvious rune pairing is found by arranging the runes in a circle and looking for the rune directly opposite (180 degrees in mathematical terms and +12 in terms of the Elder Futhark). It makes no difference whether we start at FE or at UR, their "opposite rune partners" remain unchanged. *(For a visual I refer you back to the rune wheel illustration in Chapter 1.)*

Here they are: *Polar pairs*

	(+12)	
1. Ur		13. Eoh
2. Thurs		14. Algiz
3. Ass		15. Sol
4. Reid		16. Tyr
5. Ken		17. Bjarka
6. Gifu		18. Eh
7. Wynja		19. Madr
8. Hagal		20. Lagu
9. Naud		21. Ing
10. Is		22. Odal
11. Jara		23. Dagaz
12. Perthra		24. Fe

There is an alternative order where EOH and PERTHRA swap around and where ODAL and DAGAZ also trade places. This obviously affects the *polar pairs,* therefore:

Polar pairs (version #2)

1. Ur (+12)	13. Perthra *(Eoh)*
2. Thurs	14. Algiz
3. Ass	15. Sol
4. Reid	16. Tyr
5. Ken	17. Bjarka
6. Gifu	18. Eh
7. Wynja	19. Madr
8. Hagal	20. Lagu
9. Naud	21. Ing
10. Is	22. Dagaz *(Odal)*
11. Jara	23. Odal *(Dagaz)*
12. Eoh *(Perthra)*	24. Fe

FE will partner up with either EOH or with PERTHRA. JARA teams up with either DAGAZ or ODAL. One can embark on profound cosmic meditations, pondering the implications of that.

Ask yourself: *what comes first home and belonging (ODAL) or enlightenment (evolving, seeing everything from a higher perspective)?*

Rune Triads

Once you get the hang of how rune pairings operate, you will discover that powerful rune triads (and even larger groupings) exist as well. We already met some in the previous chapter. Rune pairs open (linear) continuums and rune triads (where three runes interact) open *multi-dimensional* spaces, where additional forces interact and affect fields of human experience. You could say that they cover cosmological concepts and larger, mythical, timelines.

I often use runes as shorthand in my notebooks: I discovered that many myths can be summarized as a triad of three (or four) runes.

The Dial on the Washing Machine

Working with these groupings will reveal rich layers of meaning and symbolism. *All* these correspondences work. Rune studies will never be a closed and finite body of knowledge, it will evolve as human beings evolve, paradigms shift and the world changes. Our world has already changed beyond comprehension since the Viking Age and AI will rapidly change it again. Our children would no longer recognise or understand the world of our childhood. (Mine laugh and think living before the internet was a dreadful fate!)

Think of the dial on your washing machine: turning it will select different programs. *Try all programs!* Over time you will discover which setting most resonates with you (or meets your needs). Are you a high-earning professional relying on a dry cleaner? Do you have four young children? Do you run a guesthouse and use an industrial-sized washing machine?

Also experiment with new groupings, perhaps based on correspondences sparked by your interest in another field.

Chapter Activity

Randomly pull two runes out of your pouch and meditate on their relationship. Consult Part II of this book to compare your reflections with mine. Do this as a daily practice for a set period (commit to a calendar month for instance).

Look at a situation or challenge in your life, right now, and express it in the form of a rune relationship.

Pull a rune on one question (for yourself or another person) and interpret it. Then look at the runes that precede and follow this rune. Interpret them too. Next look at its "polar opposite" and add yet another dimension of interpretation.

Chapter 6

Mythology for Rune Magicians

"Not to have known
The Gods they fear, adds terror"

Lucan, The Civil War (Pharsalia)[1]

Jane Ellen Harrison (1850 – 1928) was a British scholar of classics and a linguist. Along with Karl Kerenyi and Walter Burket she was one of the founders of modern studies in Ancient Greek religion and mythology. Her work and ideas remain remarkably fresh by today's standards. Her work was very helpful to me, while writing this chapter.

Harrison pointed out that the North Sea peoples travelled far and wide, well before the Vikings who inherited their tradition and craftsmanship. This is supported by the number of ships we see in Bronze Age petroglyphs on the west coast of Sweden.

> Once awake to this northern element in Homer we are no longer surprised to find his Olympus a certain forecast, as it were, of the atmosphere of the Eddas. The gods of Homer [...] are, in part, northerners.[2]

Of Gods, Doubles, and Impostors

In popular mythology straight comparisons are often made between the Greek deities and the Norse pantheon. This was common practice in the early days of Nordic studies. Today academics operate very stringent standards and no longer share (what amounts to) wild flights of fancy.

Just as Freyja and Frigg are *not* the same goddess (even if they shared common ancestry in Nerthus), I do *not* equate the Greek gods with their Roman counterparts, as they are all unique beings and numinous forces.

However, as this chapter concerns itself with identifying *common* (archetypal) themes, I will provide a list of perceived correspondences (or similarities).

The Sequence Followed Here Is: Greek God – Roman Equivalent – Norse Deity

- Aphrodite – Venus – Some aspects of Freyja and some aspects of Frigg
- Apollo – Phoebus Apollo – Balder, aspects of Ullr
- Ares – Mars – Tyr
- Artemis – Diana – Skadi, but only to some extent
- Athena – Minerva – Freyja
- Demeter – Ceres – Some aspects of Frigg and some aspects of Sif
- Dionysus – Bacchus – Some aspects of Freyr, not a strong link
- Eros – Cupid – lacks a Norse equivalent but Freyja is viewed as the goddess of love (and death) and Frigg as a goddess of fertility, marriage and domestic peace
- Gaia – Tellus and later Terra Mater – Jord (Fjorgyn)
- Hades – Pluto – Hel, female deity, opposite gender
- Hebe – Juventas – Idunn
- Hecate – Trivia – Skadi (tentative connection)
- Hephaestus – Vulcan – Volundr, also the Dwarfs as blacksmiths
- Hera – Juno – Frigg, also aspects of Sif
- Hermes – Mercury – Odin, with some aspects of both Loki and Heimdallr
- Nix – Nox – Nótt
- Pan – Faunus – Closest Nordic region equivalent is Finnish god Tapio

- Poseidon – Neptune – Njordr, Aegir
- Zeus – Jupiter – Thor

Further Correspondences:

- Apollo and Artemis were twins, just like Freyr and Freyja
- Fates – Parcae – Nornir (The Norns)
- Kerberos – Cerberus – Fenris
- Prometheus (known to both Greeks and Romans): Loki

Myth and the Human Imagination

Harrison observed that in animals, action follows instinct immediately but in human beings there is (usually) *a pause,* an interval between perception and action:

> 'It is in this interval that our *ideas,* our images arise. We do not instantly get what we want, so we figure to ourselves our need, and out of these images so created, which are, as it were, the empty shadows of desire, our whole mental life is built up. If reaction were instantaneous, we should have no image, no representation, practically no mental life. Religion might have had ritual, but it would have been barren of mythology.'

Emotionally and spiritually speaking this is also the space where humans can pause and choose their response to a difficult situation (as opposed to reacting automatically or impulsively).

Her second observation is that the Greeks were supreme *ikonists* (image makers) and this is one reason why their mythology lives on today. It is very important to note that they worshipped not gods, not *dei,* but powers, *numina.* These *numin*a were only dim images of activities; they never attained to personality, they had no attributes, no life histories; in a word: no mythology.[3]

Harrison's third observation is that *Homer is singing of divinities who are, in part at least, "other men's gods".*[4]

> The Olympians dwell on Olympus, a mountain on Thessaly, from which they take their name. They are Northerners. The Hellenes, who worshipped them, were an immigrant people, who came down from the valley of the Danube and conquered the indigenous Pelasgians. Homer's Achaeans are but one offshoot of those tribes of northern warriors [...] p.7
>
> -Jane Ellen Harrison p.8[5] *[Slightly abbreviated by the author]*

All gods have *an elemental form.* This is important to remember when people debate whether Thor has a beard or what Freyja's hair colour is. Those formidable beings are *an ancient elementary force engaging in visual and perceptive patterning* (in order to engage with human minds). They will appear in a way that is tailor-made for us, meaning the way that you see them (with your inner eye, so clearly and convincingly) is different from the way I see them. And that is OK. The spirit world is not the earth world of consensual reality.

This chapter maps my exploration of potent liminal zones which exist between the runes. These places describe myths and host and archetypal characters. Note that these spaces exist between *any two runes,* not just runes positioned next to each other.

A Runic Expedition Focussed on Myth

We will now travel around the wheel of the runes again. The runes of the Elder Futhark are building blocks of mythology. The process works both ways: mythology can show us hidden dimensions of the runes, but in return the runes (and rune axes) can reveal deeper layers embedded in mythology.

C.G. Jung might express this as follows: both runes and myths interact (or intersect) in the archetypal realm. They reveal blueprints wired into human consciousness (no matter what our ethnic or cultural background is). Please note that I to name those blueprints accurately I have used beings from a variety of mythologies (not only Norse).

While reading this chapter, continuously ask yourself: what is that story that any sequence or cluster of runes tells?

UR

Audhumbla is the primordial cow. We assume that Ymir drank her milk. There is an abundance of cow goddesses in mythology and sacred cows are revered in India today.

Ancient Egyptians venerated Bat, a Cow Goddess associated with the Milky Way. She was often depicted as a human face with cow ears and horns. Worship of Bat may have its origin in late Palaeolithic cattle herding cultures (FE).[6]

Most commonly she appears as a celestial cow, surrounded by stars. Her name means something akin to *feminine potency* or *the ensouled one*, or perhaps in more conceptual terms, the power of manifestation itself.[7]

The Egyptians also knew Hathor, an ancient goddess known as the Mistress of Heaven. Perceived as a celestial cow, her four legs supported the vault of heaven. Her star-spangled belly was the sky itself. She protected women during pregnancy and childbirth. As a goddess of fertility and moisture, she was also associated with the inundation of the Nile.[8]

Rune UR is the Void or Cosmic Womb, found in cosmologies all over the world.

Liminal Zone Between UR – THURS

This is the space of Twinning and Doubles. The Roman God Janus (our month January is named for him), is two-faced. Here we encounter The Other and Others – the Not Self or Not Me (which is one gift of Duality and Polarity). To do so safely human beings need healthy boundaries.

Our guide for this thorny place is the Hermaphrodite-Trickster (who usually shows up as a profoundly ambiguous God or Spirit). Loki is the trickster among Norse deities, but Odin also tricks others to gain knowledge (and the Mead of Poetry). The guardian of this space is Ymir.

THURS

Many global origin myths speak of an early race of giants, preceding human beings. Ymir is the primordial giant of Norse cosmology and an intersex being. Ymir produced offspring by themselves. Ymir's name is derived from the ON word *ymr*: an uttering or sound. It appears to refer to a primordial loud sound, or sound of creation, *a scream*. Ymir is dismembered (by Odin and his brothers, Villi and Ve) and the primordial sound shatters into a plethora of individual voices and tunes. The Aesir gods were *ljoðasmiðir* or song smiths.[9]

From Ymir's body our current world (or Universe), was created. Ymir is the first being to die and by dying becomes a life-giving force (his dismemberment allows other creatures or beings to come into existence). Ymir has been linked to Yama in the Vedic tradition: the Lord of the realm of Death, the Ruler of the Departed. The word Yama means twin and he has a twin sister called Yami. The first being to die becomes the Ruler of the (Land of the) Dead. This is the creation of *duality*.THURS is the rune of polarity and duality, of apparent contradiction. The duality is resolved through death: the return to a state of unity consciousness (DAGAZ). Between them, these runes create spaces for learning and evolving.

Incarnation on Earth confines humans to duality. Perhaps one core wound (currently being embodied and expressed by the gender dysphoria of Transgender people) is that the vast majority of us are born in either a male or female body.

Biologically speaking, conception assigns us a gender. About six weeks after fertilization an embryo develops distinct male or female genitalia. *Perhaps this brings a loss of what did not unfold? The road not travelled?*

The Anglo-Saxons viewed rune THURS as a *thorn*. It cuts the umbilical cord at birth. It also brings risk, danger and wounding. We need protection. Norse god Thors is forever "fighting giants" (the forces of chaos).

In Greek mythology Apollo and Artemis are described as both twins and healers. One major THURS teaching is *"That which divides must also learn about healing and returning to wholeness"*. Thor is an herbalist. THURS is the rune of *Dialectic Process.*

THURS – ASS

Starting at THURS and moving (clockwise) along the wheel of the runes we get the following sequence: THURS – ASS – GIFU. This triad of runes narrates how the elementary power of thunder (a divine being visualised as having control over the weather), THURS, becomes a god force (ASS). The next development is the sacred marriage (GIFU) of deities. Even gods seek companions and alliances.

Here deities walk between worlds. They guard boundaries and crossroads. They help us navigate the shadowlands between Life and Death.

Odin has a dark (or frightening) side too, as a psychopomp and chooser of the slain. He breaks oaths and abandons women he has slept with. His quest for knowledge and wisdom makes him ruthless.

ASS

ASS is *the god rune*, of Divinity and of Odin. In terms of world mythology, it is the rune of all deities or god forces; of divine inspiration, poetic frenzy and ecstatic work. It points at the altered states of consciousness which takes us, human beings, into the realm and presence of deities.

ASS – REID

At REID the Wheel of Time starts turning. Timekeepers and deities representing time live here. Having experienced the primal trauma of separation, the human soul craves "spiritual technology" for returning to the state of ecstasy: poetry, songs, chants, music etc. This is the origin of all creative pursuits, sacred art and spirit-led process. The remedy for incarnation is incantation.

REID

REID is the rune of riding. Things get moving: circles and cycles, stories and songs, music and rhythm. The first rhythm we ever experience is the heartbeat of our mother, in the womb.

It represents the wagons of the gods: wheels, chariots, the coach travelling on the Milky Way (*Helvegen*) to the Land of the Dead, transporting the souls of the deceased.

Ultimately REID is the rune of the Divinity called Time. She holds space for our human experiences and learning. REID facilitates evolution.

REID – KEN

To make our way in the world we need both transport and tools. We use wheels and speak of "reinventing the wheel".

The guardian of this space is Prometheus. He steals fire and gifts it to human beings, not only literally, but also symbolically in the form of knowledge and technology.

Arthur C. Clarke is often quoted in this context: "Any sufficiently advanced technology is indistinguishable from magic."

KEN

KEN is a pine torch. It represents things that erupt, ignite or come to the surface.

It is also the forge. KEN's indwelling spirit or divinity is a blacksmith.

The blacksmith and the shaman are of one nest, says a proverb of the Kolyma district in Siberia. *The smith is the elder brother of the shaman* is another saying from the same location.[10]

> As for the Buryats [in the Asian region of Siberia], blacksmiths and shamans always go hand in hand: the shaman protects the blacksmith and his craft, conducts blacksmith ceremonies. In his turn, the blacksmith makes metal shamanistic accessories and articles of the shaman's clothes, which protect him when he travels from one world to the other.[11]

KEN – GIFU

In both Norse and Greek mythology, we find a pairing of a blacksmith and a beautiful goddess. We also find this pairing in mythology from other continents and in fairy tales, such as the Beauty and the Beast.

When Aphrodite joined the (patriarchal) world of Mount Olympus, she was allocated Hephaistos as her husband. I sense a deeper mystery here because the Eddas report that Freyja slept with four dwarves (named Dvalinn, Grer, Berling and Alfrik) to obtain her magical necklace called Brisingamen (the name means necklace of amber or fire).[12]

The four dwarfs are the guardians of this zone. They forge many things: alliances, power objects and gifts.

GIFU

GIFU means gift or reciprocity. It can also refer to a sacred marriage. Norse material hints at a sacred marriage occurring between the most powerful god and a Völva, a seeress (think of Thor and Sif or Odin and Frigg).

> *Studies initiated by the Norwegian academic Gro Steinsland have shown that many skaldic poems describe human lineages descended from a sacred marriage between a (Norse) god and a*

giantess. This was a key concept in the spiritual belief system of the Vikings and Viking Age people.[13]

Harrison observed that the amount of hostility and strife in the Zeus-Hera marriage indicates that Hera was coerced, but never really subdued, by an alien conqueror. She was forced into marriage, as an ancient Pelasgian divinity.[14]

The shadow side of GIFU: a forced marriage or abusive marriage, coercive control.

GIFU – WYNJA

This space holds the fruits of a happy marriage or, in the agricultural cycle, a well-tended farm or homestead delivering good harvests.

The guardian of this domain is Frigg. She brings the blessings of a well-run orderly home, filled with love and laughter, prosperity and security. Kvilhaug reminds us that both Frigg and Gefjon are described as knowing the fate of all beings. At Rune ASS we found ecstatic work and here we find prophecy (ecstatic work on behalf of the community).[15]

WYNJA

WYNJA expresses domestic peace and contentment. It indicates a winning streak and Frigg's influence. The Old Norse people performed a blót at specific times of the year. The verb *blóta* means *to worship, by means of (animal) blood sacrifice.* After the sprinkling of sacrificial blood, three toasts were drunk, one to Odin for victory, one to Njord for wealth, and one to Freyr for frith.

In contemporary Swedish, two different words have evolved from the Old Norse word *friðr*. The first one is *fred* (peace, as in a state where is no war or conflict, referring to an external situation) and *frid* (an internal state, peace of mind).

A related expression exists, of things being "fredat/fredad", literally "peaced" (less literally: left in peace). It refers to things having untouchable and protected status: animals that may not be hunted, flowers that may not be picked, land that cannot be developed.

WYNJA – HAGAL

We are catapulted from balance and contentment into a full-blown crisis, but crisis is also opportunity or turning point. The guardian of this space is the Norn Skuld. Her name means Debt. She never fails to serve us karmic payment requests (as it were). There is always more balancing to be done. We can't stagnate in contentment for too long.

HAGAL

HAGAL brings a crisis, sudden cataclysmic change or initiation. It is the unexpected hailstorm that destroys the crops. For Norse rune magicians it is also the Rune of Witches. One of their jobs was defending crops from bad weather. However, if a local witch diverts hail, where does it go? The neighbouring community! The damage done by hail, heralds the advent of NAUD, the rune of need and dire necessity.

HAGAL – NAUD

We yield to Necessity as the Mother of Invention. We tighten our belt. The resident Guardian is the "Kärring" (SW), the Crone, who holds the key to the secrets of resurrection and rebirth.[16]

NAUD

Naud is the rune of Need, Necessity and the Norns. We come up against the fate they carve for us. We encounter restriction, limitation, necessity and all things inevitable. We experience profound frustration.

NAUD – IS

This place marks the transition from acute crisis to being becalmed. We yield and accept restriction. We stop moving for a while (REID –

IS). After a pause we strap on skis (or snowshoes) and start moving around the changed landscape. We adapt. If we can't change our circumstances, we change ourselves and our expectations.

Norse Winter Goddess Skaði is the Guardian of this cold frozen zone. Her name is derived from an Old Norse word for damage or harm and intrinsically linked to shadow. The cataclysm of HAGAL also means that some souls do not see the light of a new day. The Norns cut their thread of life and they die a literal death. Their souls continue their journey in otherworld realms.

IS

Deep winter brings introspection. The Norns carve the fate of all beings but what role do we play in the fate of others? Are we a blessing or burden in the lives of others? Is brings time on Ice: reflection and gazing at unflattering mirrors. The deep-frozen period of transparency can help us reach hard-won clarity. When things freeze and all movement stops, we can see deep into the heart of any matter.

IS – JARA

Here things start moving again. The ice has melted. Seeds can be planted, ensuring a future harvest. The Guardians of this zone are the frost giants. Between ice and harvest we navigate a dialectic process, a sacred marriage of opposites. The resulting tension stretches us, educates us, makes grow and evolve. We protect tender seeds from night frost. We grow in the process.

JARA

A popular Norse toast was *Til árs ok friðar*: *for a good harvest and frith or peace.* JARA is the rune of the Harvest (literally of the year, completion, a cycle coming full circle). Harrison described the Greek Goddess Hera as *the daimon who brings the fruits of the year in their season* with a three-fold seasonal aspect:

- Child/Maiden
- (Married) Full-grown
- (Separated from her Husband) Chera (the Desolate One).

Literally the classical Greek word *chera* (χηρα) means *widow* but in modern times we no longer define women by their relationships to men or by motherhood status. In my way of thinking the moder Chera is a Wise Woman or Crone, a sovereign force.

Jara marks the point where a seed (ING) has been planted, watered, tended, fully grown and is eventually harvested. The plant then produces *its own seeds* and the cycle repeats.

JARA – PERTHRA

After the harvest we retreat into the cave of the Mountain Mother. Cave time prepares us for starting a new cycle, forever changed by the ordeal we survived at HAGAL. The guardian of this zone is the Bergsrå (SW) or Great Mountain Spirit, notorious for spiriting people away into the mountains.

PERTHRA

For Nordic rune magicians PERTHRA is the rune of rocks, where the tomb mystically equals the womb. Here something is sheltered during a time of gestation or incubation before it emerges back into the world and sees daylight. The PERTRHA – SOL axis paints a vision of Sunna rising every morning from the Underworld (below the horizon), casting beams of sunlight into caves and caverns.

PERTHRA – EOH

In a cave near world tree Yggdrasil, new life gestates while the world turns on her axis. A "spiritual baby" (a new worldview, project or self) floats in amniotic waters (Urðarbrunnr, the Well of Urðr), *awaiting birth and daylight. The guardian of his zone is Yggdrasil. The guardians of this zone are the Eagle (unnamed) at the top of the tree and Níðhöggr (the dragon or serpent gnawing on the roots of the tree).*

EOH

The world tree is a key theme in several religions and mythologies (especially Indo-European religions, Siberian beliefs and some Native American belief systems). It connects all worlds. Its branches touch the heavens, and its roots reach the underworld.

EOH – ALGIZ

This is woodland where extinct tree species still exist. It includes "the forest on the bottom of the sea". Doggerland was once a large area of land, now submerged by the North Sea. The great Hercynian Forest once covered uch of northern Europe.[17]

This ancient woodland is inhabited by antlered beings and hybrids. The Wild One patrols this territory. The Christianisation of Europe turned this untameable being (the Heart of the Wild) into "the Devil" (complete with horns and hoofs). His predecessors were Pan and Cernunnos. Their green blood runs in his veins as rising sap.

ALGIZ

The Moose Rune (*älg* in Swedish) is also the rune of the animal kingdom. Visually speaking ALGIZ could be perceived as a crow's foot or swan in flight. Here we find all horned gods and antlered beings: the Lord of the Game, the Mistress of Animals, the Lord of Wild Animals, Elen of the Ways, The Reindeer Mother, Cernunnos, Pan etc. In rock art we find therianthropes and antlered beings, possibly shamans merging with animal spirits.

ALGIZ – SOL

Sami stories speak of a Reindeer Mother carrying the returning sun in her antlers, at the winter solstice. They believe that the Creator placed a reindeer heart at the very centre of creation.[18]

This zone is the domain of Reindeer Mother. Reindeer mate in the autumn, and male reindeer shed their antlers at mating time. At the time of the winter solstice all antler-bearing reindeer are female. It is also the realm of the dragon-serpents of Norse cosmology: Níðhǫggr, Jǫrmungandr and Fafnir. This place offers uncomfortable teachings about all the ways that predator and prey interact, in a cosmic dance.

SOL

SOL is the rune of the Sun. In Norse mythology she is Sunna, a *female* giantess. From a mythological point of view the Sun rises daily (and visually) from below the horizon, from a cave or dark place inside the Earth. In summer she reaches her zenith. In the Northern European winter, she does not rise very high (or indeed *at all*, above the Arctic Circle).

SOL – TYR

Sunna illuminates the transition from a Wild God to the Spiritual Warrior. We are socialized out of being feral or living completely in the moment. We anticipate and plan. Following in Tyr's footsteps, we prioritise others (or the community) over self. We hear an echo of Prometheus. This space throws up moral dilemmas and difficult choices.

The guardian is Álfröðull (Old Norse for elf-beam or elf-glory), a common kenning (condensed metaphor) for Sunna and her chariot. The poem Vafþrúðnismál prophesies that Álfröðull will give birth to a daughter. A wolf will devour Sunna (SOL) at Ragnarok, but her daughter will continue to circle the heavens. The "Daughter of the Sun" constitutes a promise about the continuation of life on Earth, beyond our personal death and even in a new world, after Ragnarok.[19]

TYR

TYR is the arrow-shaped rune of Norse god Tyr, the spiritual warrior.

The Fenris wolf (prophesied to kill Odin during Ragnarok) was only a pup but growing fast. The gods decided to tie up Fenrir with a magical fetter from which he couldn't escape. When Fenris saw the chain and became suspicious. He allowed the gods to fetter him, but only if one of them put an arm in his mouth (as a pledge of good faith). Only Tyr volunteered. Fenris bit off Tyr's arm (or hand).

Tyr became the one-armed god, also a god of oaths and vows. In Lokasenna, trickster god Loki insults the Norse goddesses, accusing them of infidelity, and he tells Tyr: "You can't be the right hand of justice among the people!" humiliating Tyr for his missing right hand.[20]

Rune TYR can be viewed as an arrow pointing at the Pole Star. The story of the lost arm may indicate that Tyr lost a more prominent place due to axial precession.

TYR – BJARKA

Here we meet the female counterpart of Tyr: the female spiritual warrior.

We generally think of soldiers and warriors as male, but archaeologists have excavated grave sites of Norse women warriors.

The guardians of this space are the Shield Maidens. There is debate about whether they were historical figures or not, but the archaeologist Neil Price showed that a 10th century burial on the Swedish island of Birka, excavated in the 1870s and assumed to contain a male turned out to belong to a female Viking warrior![21]

BJARKA

BJARKA is the rune of the birch tree and motherhood. Norse material does not back up (or preserve) the mother signification, but an abundance of Slavic material and sauna traditions in Finland and Russia do. In magical work birch is associated with feminine power. It was used in healing ceremonies for women and girls; also, in ritual preparation for marriage.

There plant mothers and animal mothers on Earth long before human mothers appeared. We draw strength from our relationships with them.

In some areas in Fennoscandia the birch tree was perceived as the world tree. She had a male counterpart in the Oak Tree. Both trees exist as runes (Oak tree AC is a rune in the Anglo-Saxon Futhorc). Linguists connect the Russian name for the birch tree to a verb (birch" – берёза, *beryoza*) and that verb means *to keep safe.*[22]

BJARKA – EH

This zone is inhabited by mythical or supernatural horses and by horse-headed goddesses of fertility and healing. The Horse Rune is also the rune of death and soul conductors Here fertility and death touch.

We are invited to explore the difference between medicine and poison. Paracelsus famously said: "Everything is a poison, nothing is a poison. It is the dose that makes the poison".

Tyr betrays Fenris lost his arm (or hand). Unsurprisingly the next rune is Bjarka, the Healer!

We learn how to harness wolf power. We subdue the wolf within ourselves, but this comes at a cost, at a wound to our soul. At regular intervals we need re-wilding and going feral. What are we greedy for?

Rune GIFU sits opposite EH on the rune wheel, which indicates a strong relationship between the gift (of Life) and the ultimate "taking away" (Death). Paradoxically Death also bestows gifts (inheritances and acquiring "other people's money"). The guardians of this zone are the Nine Maidens (Disir) of the Mountain of Healing (Lyfjaberg).[23]

Rune EH

Horse Rune and Rune of Partnership

EH

This rune looks exactly like a capital letter M but it has nothing to do with that letter. It is more helpful to see it as either a horse or two horses (representing twins and partnership).

Sleipnir presides over the Horse Rune. He was born to trickster god Loki so he has a male mother.

We live in a time of genderfluidity, revisioning gender constructs, and gay couples having families through IVF and surrogacy. This zone offers rick pickings for modern practitioners.

The rune of the *psychopomp* (soul conductor), twins and partnership teaches us to move seamlessly between the worlds.

The *Helhest* (Horse of goddess Hel) reportedly only has three legs. It appears in many of 19th century Danish phrases. *Helhest* takes the Norse goddess Hel anywhere in Midgard to collect the souls of the dead.

Árvakr (early awake) and *Alsviðr* (very swift) are the horses which pull the chariot of the sun (SOL) across the sky each day.

Wild horses were domesticated during the Stone Age. Initially they were hunted as food. Later they were tamed as working animals and beasts of burden. Over time horses became companions and a powerful ally in wars.

EH – MADR

This is the domain of the Alcis, a pair of Divine Twins described by Tacitus. He described them as horse gods, though the Latin word alces refers to elks or moose, so there is some ambiguity. Twin gods often appear in the roles of rescuers, healers and protectors in other Indo-European mythologies. Here horse and rider are as one: we learn about merging with animal powers.

MADR

The rune of human beings and the human condition is also the rune of the Ancestors (all human beings that ever lived) and Descendants (all those who come after us).

MADR – LAGU

This zone holds all close connections between human beings and water and all guardians patrolling bodies of water. In the medieval literature and mythology surrounding King Arthur we find references to a Lady of the Lake.

Nerthus lives on here, but there are other guardians too, such as the Margygr. This Old Norse word translates as Sea Giantess (or Sea Spirit). She can be beautiful and helpful, but also malevolent (even violent). She is sometimes called a Water-Wife.[24]

Móðguðr watches over the Gjallarbrú, (the bridge over the river Gjöll, leading to the Land of the Dead). Powerful human-fish hybrids live here too, such as sirens, mermaids and selkies. The most powerful guardian of all is Jǫrmungandr, the world serpent, who lives on the bottom of the ocean and bites its own tail, thus holding our world securely together.

LAGU

LAGU is the rune of water in all its manifestations. The human body consists of about 50-65% water, which reflects the same water-land proportion as Earth. Blood is one manifestation of LAGU. This territory holds all things we associate with water: emotions, going with the flow, creative flow, memories and emotions etc. Religious significations for LAGU are rebirth (baptism) and purification (ritual baths).

There is a rune for the Sun (SOL) but not for the Moon. As the Moon exerts an influence on water (tides, menstruation etc.), LAGU is the runic dimension where we find the Moon.

LAGU – ING

Seeds need watering to germinate and release their full potential. Also think of semen, sexuality and sexual intercourse. The guardians of this zone are the Nine Mothers of Heimdallr. Those nine (mysterious) sisters gave birth to one son together. They may (or may not) be identical to the Nine Wave Maidens. We find a couple trying for a baby on the Rune Triad MADR – LAGU – ING.

ING

ING is the rune of Norse god Freyr, twin brother of Freyja. It is literally an abstract representation of a seed and by extension the rune of sexuality and reproduction. Watery semen carries life-giving power. A foetus floats in amniotic fluid during pregnancy.

ING – ODAL

Sexuality secures offspring. A child needs a safe home. ING is followed by ODAL. In this zone we find a family homestead and its descendants, where the descendants sit in the shade of the trees planted by the ancestors, (the EOH – MADR – ING – ODAL QUARTET).

The Guardians of this space are the Alfar (male ancestors who remain connected to homestand and farmland) and the Tompteghud (Spirit of house and property).

ODAL

The old word *Tompth* means a defined piece of land in which a house is located. Another old name for a new building is *Bol* and the tomte was sometimes called *Bol-vaette* in the old days. From "tomt" and "bo" the concept of *Tomtebo-luck* is found.[25]

ODAL is the rune of safe enclosed space and the (ancestral) homestead. It refers to our homebase, our sanctuary. In our day people often move around. Most of us no longer have an ancestral home (in a specific location).

In rune readings ODAL can also refer to the country we live in, or the place we call home, even if we do not live there. It can even represent our homeland.

The 14th century Saint Birgitta complained vociferously about the importance people attributed to their "*Tomptha-Gud*" (an old Swedish word referring to the *Tomte* as a deity).

The general concept is that the first person to die in a house becomes its *tomte* (House Spirit, SW) after death, but a change of the guards is always possible. A house without a *tomte* is vulnerable and an angry or resentful *tomte* is even worse. He can block luck and play unpleasant pranks on the inhabitants.[26] Besides appearing in human shape (in visions or dreams) the *tomte* can also shapeshift into a snake. These snakes are called usually called *Tomt-orm (CS "snake of the property").*

They are fed with milk and used to be venerated in most parts of Scandinavia (very much like the *žaltys* in Lithuania). Killing such a snake would mean that one risked losing all the accumulated luck (*hamingja* ON) of a place.

ODAL – DAGAZ

Powerful learning occurs when we leave home. Assuming that home was a happy place, we now step outside the loving protection of that enclosure. In leaving a very dysfunctional or unhappy home, we may experience an exhilarating sense of freedom instead. We distance ourselves from emotional enmeshment. In both cases a mirroring occurs: we come face to face with ourselves. In the highest possible outcome, ancestral insights and healing can happen. Illumination brings shifts in awareness.

The Guardians of this zone are the Disir, the deified maternal ancestors (the female counterpart of the Alfar).

DAGAZ

DAGAZ IS light in a metaphysical and symbolic sense, while SOL is the material sun (a celestial body). Key words are illumination, enlightenment, a higher level of perception or awareness, paradigm shifts.

DAGAZ – FE

We see a glimpse of eternity. We are not immortal on an individual level, but we have lived and learned. We may believe in the continuation of consciousness after death. The Poetic Edda speaks of another world, after Ragnarok.

It describes a settled life and enlightened mindset. Traversing this zone might make us charitable or altruistic, following the principles of right action and community spirit. The guardian of this space is the Norse god Baldr, son of Odin and Frigg. Baldr had frightening dreams, foretelling his death. Frigg extracted a promise from all beings not to harm him, except mistletoe. The gods then amuse themselves by throwing things at him. Loki fashions an arrow from mistletoe wood and helps Baldr's own blind brother, Höðr, throw it at him. Baldr dies and now lives with Hel in Helheim.

Baldr represents the promise of enlightenment and a new world when our current one ends. This is why he is safe in Hel (not Valhalla). He will not fight at Ragnarok but return once Ragnarok ends.

FE

FE is the first rune of the Futhark but the final rune of the Uthark. We come full circle. We prepare for "another journey around the wheel".

Most of us don't own cattle. FE asks us to reflect on fair energy exchange (a theme started at GIFU) and the value we place on our own (and other people's) time and efforts. In our day of environmental awareness FE also flags the issue of "the true value and cost of things" (from air travel to disposable plastic bottles).

FE – UR

Between FE and UR we find the continuum between the feral aurochs and cattle. We reflect on how we have been "tamed", what needs re-wilding. The guardians of this space are our berserker-ancestors.

Chapter 7

Wheels Within Wheels
(The Runes and Astrology)

Let me start by presenting the key assumptions which underpin the chapters about astrology and astronomy (viewed through a Norse lens):

1. The Vikings were master navigators, but they have not left us written documentation of any astro-navigation techniques they used to sail the seas.
2. There is no evidence that Old Norse people practiced astrology.
3. There is no evidence either that they connected the runes to (or derived the runes from) star patterns in the night sky.
4. Many (other) early scripts have been linked to star patterns and the star constellations of earlier times.
5. The sources tell us about some patterns the Old Norse people saw in the night sky. They do not resemble the star constellations of modern Western Culture.
6. The *Poetic Edda* contains many references to astronomical numbers and concepts. This suggests a strong connection to astronomy (and other ancient texts, such as the Indian Vedas).
7. The poem *Grímnismál* offers a description of the twelve Houses or domains of the Norse Gods. The (Western) Zodiac also has twelve houses.
8. The poem *Alvíssmál* provides the names Old Norse people gave to celestial bodies.

Does Astrology Have a Place in This Book?

Western astrology has its roots in the period around 500 BCE, when the concept of a zodiac with twelve houses was developed by the Chaldeans. The foundations of the astrological methods used today were laid down in the Hellenistic period in Greece. We have access to material written by Egyptian, Babylonian and Semitic astrologers. There was a blending of astrology and Hermetic ideas. Astrology then reached India via the Middle East, where Vedic Astrology developed. The Qabala dates from the same period.

Before the Enlightenment (or Age of Reason) there was no distinction between chemistry and *alchemy*, between mathematics and *numerology*, between astronomy and *astrology* etc. What modern people perceive as reputable fields within science acquired a "shadow twin we ridicule". This split into duality and *othering* is a Rune THURS phenomenon.

The Old Norse peoples, based on everything we know, did not practice astrology. Therefore, it can be argued strongly that this material has no place in a book about the runes. However, based on key discoveries from the field of archeoastronomy, we do need to look at this material *but on a level of key lenses of observation operating in contemporary Western Civilisation, not in terms of authentic Old Norse studies.*

This chapter cannot begin to give a proper introduction to astrology but there are many excellent sources on the market. I will present only the bare bones needed to present my reasoning in the two subsequent chapters.

Reading Patterns

What both astrology and the runes have in common is that they *involve reading patterns.* And those patterns have a degree of predictability because they follow cycles (REID). The dominant cycle here in Midgard (the Earth world of matter) involves *the cycle of Life-Death-Rebirth* on many different levels (from cells, animals and humans to businesses, political eras and entire civilizations). In contrast, the parallel cycle in the Other World (the "World-Outside -Time", astral world, spirit world or energetic parallel realm) appears to be focussed on *cycles of evolution of consciousness and soul.*

Modern physics has discovered many fascinating phenomena. Two such examples are *fractals* and *quantum entanglement.* Perhaps we modern people are moving closer to the ancient world view, where all things were perceived as interconnected and meaningful, not a large collection of random events.

Fractals

A fractal is an ever-repeating pattern. Fractals are infinitely complex patterns that are self-similar across different scales. They are created by repeating a simple process over and over in an ongoing feedback loop. Fractals abound in nature: trees, rivers, coastlines, mountains, clouds, seashells, hurricanes. Abstract fractals – such as the Mandelbrot Set – can be generated by a computer, calculating a simple equation over and over.[1]

Quantum Entanglement

Quantum entanglement means that two or multiple particles are linked together in such a way that the measurement of one particle's quantum state determines the possible quantum states of the other particles. This connection doesn't depend on the location of the particles in space. Even if you separate entangled particles by billions of miles, changing one particle will induce a change in the other. Even though quantum entanglement[2] appears to transmit information instantaneously, it doesn't violate the classical speed of light because there is *no movement through space.*

The speed of light is "the speed limit of our universe", but it only applies to *items that have mass*. In plain English: the state of one particle is affected by another particle, lightyears away. Might the same thing be true for human beings? Do the runes point us in that direction?

Nigel Pennick wrote a fascinating book about the runes and astrology[3] (a new edition was published in 2023) in which he explored runic time cycles and how they align with both the seasons and the stars (cosmic patterning). He introduced the concepts of a runic year and runic hours. He explained the significance of the planets and fixed stars and offers a template for a runic birth chart.

Divination

The runes are commonly used in divination (but there are many other applications). Many people also think of astrology as a system for divination, but most astrologers will challenge this. Most areas of astrology are not primarily about predicting or forecasting. Like the runes, astrology can only identify trends and patterns, not guarantee outcomes.

The runes interact with the patterning (interests, personality, character, previous choices) that make up the totality that is YOU, but they also read the larger collective field. In astrology your natal chart is perceived as "a map of your soul".

Relationships Between Runes

I asked myself: *can the ancient art of astrology teach us something about the Wheel of the Runes, especially about the relationships between the runes (through a modern lens, not an Old Norse one)?*

In terms of connecting the 24 runes of the Elder Futhark to the 12 signs of the Zodiac my next research questions were:

- What are the origins of the alphabet?
- Do some alphabets or writing systems have a connection to the night sky?

These questions led me to the work of Brian R. Pellar[4] (see the Appendix with the Recommended Reading list).

The Runes and the Zodiac

The Wheel of the Runes and the Zodiac both provide a time-tested sequence for the unfolding of cosmic and natural cycles. Those (telescopic and microscopic) templates help us see what happened before and what will likely happen next. They can help us make decisions about *dancing with possibilities*.

The Sun and Moon follow a very specific (and narrowly defined) path across the sky. This track is called the ecliptic. The twelve constellations through which the ecliptic passes form the Zodiac together. The ecliptic runs exactly along the middle of the Zodiac.[5]

As Earth spins on her axis, the twelve houses of the zodiac appear to spin around us, overhead. Whatever sign is rising over the eastern horizon at a given time, is the *rising sign* and will appear as such in the natal chart of any individual born at that time.

The Zodiac represents the path of the Sun across the sky (as seen from Earth). Astrology divides this "belt" into 12 houses (like cutting a pie or pizza into 12 slices):

> *"The planets are the characters, the signs are the costumes they're wearing, and the houses are the stages (or areas of life) where they're lived out".*[6]

The first sign of the Zodiac, Aries, responds to the first house (but they are not identical) and so forth. Just as the twelve signs of the Zodiac (moving from 1 – 12), tell the story of evolutionary development, so do the twelve houses (seen in meaningful succession).

The adventure of incarnation on Earth starts at Aries, which is all about self-awareness and propelling oneself forward into the world. It comes full circle at Pisces (my own sun sign) which is about deep dreaming, mysticism and the return to unity consciousness (a dissolving of the human ego).

The same evolutionary cycles play out for groups, entire cultures and (on a smaller scale) projects and events. Anything that has a lifespan will follow this pattern. Look at any astrology chart (natal or other) and you will soon see that the Houses situated opposite each other contain polarities. They naturally form pairs:

- First House: *Self* – Seventh House: *Others.*
- Second House: *personal resources and money* – Eighth House: *other people's money (also death: when we die other people inherit our earthly resources).*
- Third House: *thinking and communication on the everyday level (and short distances)* – Ninth House: *higher thinking/ perspectives/communication.*
- Fourth House: *home, private life, family* – Tenth House: *our career, professional life, colleagues.*
- Fifth House: *love/procreation/offspring* – Eleventh House: *friends, groups, communities.*
- Sixth House: *our personal health and personal service* – Twelfth House: *collective health, public service.*

Learning this helped me identify runic polar pairs.

Freyja Aswynn connects the 12 mansions of the gods, as listed in Grímnismál, to the 12 signs of the modern Zodiac.[7] She says that these "palaces" can be superimposed on the 12 astrological houses as follows:

- Himmingbjǫrg – Cancer
- Breiðablik – Leo
- Sǫkkvabekkr – Virgo

- Glitnir – Libra
- Glaðsheimr – Scorpio
- Ydalir – Sagittarius
- Landvíði – Capricorn
- Valaskjálf – Aquarius
- Nóatún – Pisces
- Bilskírnir – Aries
- Þrymheimr (Thrymheim) – Taurus
- Fólkvangr – Gemini

I have tried to match the 24 runes of the Elder Futhark to the twelve houses of astrology. I connected the significations of houses to the energy signatures of the runes. I could only express this in the form of *relationships between runes*. To achieve this, we need to look for a continuum between two or three runes (axes or triads). Here is my best attempt:

1. **House of Aries: IS – TYR** (a solidifying into self and initiating, meeting the world as a "warrior").
2. **House of Taurus: FE – ODAL – PERTHRA** (Accumulating wealth and possessions, grounded and earthy, slow-moving, root cellar).
3. **House of Gemini: ASS – WYNJA – REID** (super-curious and communicative, fast-moving but easily distracted).
4. **House of Cancer: BJARKA – LAGU** (Emotional and maternal, nurturing and sensitive, home bodies).
5. **House of Leo: SOL – IS** (Bold and dominant, as outward expressions of the "solar self", yearns for visibility and limelight, self-centred).
6. **House of Virgo: NAUD – REID** (Focus on work and duty/doing the necessary, repeated actions required to manage human existence, attention to detail, sometimes critical).

7. **House of Libra: DAGAZ – EH** (Partnerships and balancing the scales, peacekeepers and diplomats, justice and fairness, occasionally indecisive).
8. **House of Scorpio: ING – EH – THURS** (House of sex, death and taxes. Creative, secretive, drastic or morbid on occasion).
9. **House of Sagittarius: REID – HAGAL – DAGAZ** (Adventurous, lifelong travellers and truth-seekers. House of religion and spiritual crises or initiations).
10. **House of Capricorn: JARA – EOH – KEN** (High-achieving, "climbing goats", empire builders, authentic, harvesters of acclaim).
11. **House of Aquarius: MADR – GIFU** (Humanitarian rebel, progressive and innovative. Group-focussed, natural born networker).
12. **House of Pisces: LAGU – ALGIZ – UR** (Dissolving back into a state of oneness with the Divine, sacrifices and secrets, depth psychology, ecstasy and addictions, return to Divine origin).

I invite all readers (trained in astrology) to make their own (improved) version of correspondences. If you do, please share them with me.

The Planets Are Gods

The ancient Babylonians, Greeks, Persians, Romans etc. thought of the seven classical planets as gods and named their seven days of the week after them. In classical antiquity those seven planets were the seven luminaries that could be seen with the naked eye: the Moon, Mercury, Venus, the Sun, Mars, Jupiter and Saturn. *In other words, Uranus and Neptune had not yet been discovered or named – but they already existed, obviously!*

Astrologers use the word planet in a different way from astronomers. For their purposes the Sun and Moon are planets as well (moving in the sky and around charts).

Pluto used to have planet-status but was demoted to dwarf planet. Astronomers currently acknowledge eight (not nine) planets in our Solar System.

The inner, rocky, planets are Mercury, Venus, Earth and Mars. The outer planets are gas giants Jupiter and Saturn and ice giants Uranus and Neptune.

As these celestial bodies are key players, let me (tentatively) link them to Norse divinities, working our way from the Sun outward. Please note that we are naming *correspondences, not exact equivalents or personifications):*

- The Sun = Sól
- The Moon = Máni
- Mercury = Odin
- Venus = Frigg and Freyja
- Mars = Tyr
- *Asteroid Belt = Fire Giants*
- Jupiter = Thor
- Saturn = The Norns
- Uranus = Loki
- Neptune = Aegir, Njord
- *Kuiper Belt = Ice Giants*
- Pluto and Charon = Hel

Next, I will assign runes to the (traditionally used) list of nine worlds, but I do not find exact correspondences:

- Asgard (ON Ásgarðr) = ASS
- Muspelheim *(ON Múspellsheimr)* = SOL – KEN ("the Divine blacksmith causes sparks to fly in his forge").
- Vanaheim (ON *Vanaheimr*) = ING – JARA – WYNJA

- Midgard (ON Miðgarðr) = MADR
- Jotunheim (ON Jǫtunheimr) = THURS
- Niflheimr = IS
- Svartalfheim or Nidavellir (ON *Niðavellir)* = KEN – PERTHRA
- Ljusalfheim = DAGAZ
- Helheim = HAGAL

Chapter 8

Star Maps
(The Runes, the Zodiac, and Early Alphabets)

The runes of the Elder Futhark do not follow the alphabet sequence. The question posed in this chapter is: *does their order nevertheless tell a story that is in alignment with ancient alphabets?*

I will compare the Elder Futhark with the ancestors of modern alphabets to see if a consistent story emerges by means of star constellations, letters, symbols, and significations. Judith Dillon wrote a fascinating paper about alphabets and number magic (now available in book form).[1] She concluded that:

- The ordered symbols of the original alphabet (and its descendants) contain too consistent a story to have been randomly chosen and ordered.
- At its root, our alphabet is based on number magic.
- The last eight letters or glyphs may well hide mathematical or astronomical secrets.

My own conclusions are that:

- The sequence of the runes unfolds in close alignment with creation stories from all over the world.
- This alignment is more congruent when I use the Uthark sequence.
- There is also a very close connection between the sequence of the runes and sequences of core events in world mythology.
- The third Aett (family or grouping) of the runes, especially, contains astronomical references and points to larger cosmic cycles.

ABC

Creation did not happen once upon a time, in the distant past. Creation is always happening. Our own choices, actions and even unconscious motivations are contributing to this process, in every moment and location.

The ancient Greek Alphabet (α – alpha plus β – beta) gave us the term *Alphabet*. It has been used to write the Greek language since around 900 BCE. It was derived from the earlier Phoenician alphabet, and it was the first alphabetic script to have distinct letters for vowels as well as consonants. It is the ancestor of the Latin and Cyrillic scripts.[2]

The Palaeo-Hebrew alphabet was the script used in the historic kingdoms of Israel and Judea.[3] It is a variant of the Phoenician alphabet.

A Very Brief History of Writing

We take literacy for granted, living our lives through screens and using many symbols, but this was not always so. We use the *Latin alphabet* and *Arabic numerals* (1, 2, 3 etc.)[4]

Our Latin alphabet is a direct descendent of Egyptian Hieroglyphs. Writing was a late development in the history of human language. The poems in the Eddas were not written down until the 13th century, two centuries after the Christianisation of Scandinavia.

Writing was formally invented in Mesopotamia (the region of modern-day Iraq) and Egypt, about 5,500 years ago. It was also invented independently in China and Mesoamerica.

Some notational signs, positioned next to pictures of animals, may have appeared as early as the Upper Palaeolithic period in Europe (circa 35,000 BCE). That would make it the earliest example of *proto-writing*, where symbols were used in various combinations to convey seasonal or behavioural information for hunters.

The origins of writing are more commonly attributed to the start of the pottery-phase of the Neolithic, when clay tokens were used to record numbers of livestock and other commodities. Initially those tokens were pressed into clay tablets. Actual writing is first recorded in Uruk, at the end of the 4th millennium BCE.

An ancient Mesopotamian poem gives us the first known story of the invention of writing:

> Because the messenger's mouth was heavy and he couldn't repeat (the message), the Lord of Kulaba patted some clay and put words on it, like a tablet. Until then, there had been no putting words on clay.
>
> — *Sumerian epic poem Enmerkar and the Lord of Aratta. c. 1800 BCE.*[5]

The earliest scripts were neither alphabets nor pure pictograms. All Egyptian hieroglyphs represented objects from everyday life, but their meaning was complex. They followed the rebus principle and often stood for sounds (or sound combinations) instead. (An English equivalent would be a picture of a bee for the letter B). A picture of a goose could stand for the animal goose "gb", or for the sound "gb" followed by a glyph of the seated earth-god Geb.

The earliest writing systems *matched symbols to phonetic sounds*. That is an extremely economic way of writing, compared to Chinese characters. By comparison: the Table of General Standard Chinese Characters currently has 8,105 characters, with 6,500 being common. *The Great Compendium of Chinese Characters* has 54,678 characters. Compared to an alphabet, that is a lot to memorize!

This innovation (phonetic writing) created the basis for the scripts that (most) Western languages use today. The Phoenician alphabet was used to write the Early Iron Age Canaanite languages. Around 750 BC, ancient Greeks learned the alphabet from the seafaring Phoenicians and added an innovation: vowels.

Early alphabets (such as Phoenician, Ancient Hebrew and Aramaic) did not write in the vowels. People used them in spoken language but didn't indicate them in their writing. (Modern Hebrew still does not write vowels but sometimes uses dots, placed underneath/above/next to consonants, to indicate them). Therefore, the second great innovation was that the Greeks took certain letters, representing consonants which did not exist in Greek, and adapted those for writing vowel sounds instead.[6] Western languages do write in the vowels. The Elder Futhark has runes for vowels too.

In this chapter I will compare the position (*not the phonetic value*) of the runes to ancient alphabets and tell the story of the three A*ettir* in more detail.

I have included the 18 Charms from the Old Norse poem Hávamál. In *Ljóðatal* (stanzas 146–164), Odin counts up 18 charms that can protect human beings from trolls (in post-Christianization Scandinavia, the world *troll* refers to any being or external force that is not benevolent, not only supernatural beings).

#1 UR

Primordial Bovine, the Undivided One, teeming formless potential

Alphabet letter #1 is Aleph (Hebrew) or Alpha (Greek, A α).
In Hebrew the Phoenician Aleph 𐤀becomes Alef א.
In both Phoenician and ancient Hebrew, the A is tilted 90 degrees to the left: 𐤀
The Phoenician Aleph was derived from the Egyptian hieroglyph for Ox or Bull.[7]

Letter A represents the head of the celestial bull (Taurus) but also the shape of a woman's womb. In alphabets the first letter commonly represents a bovine: a primordial horned being. Auðumbla (UR) suckles primordial giant Ymir (THURS).

Hávamál, 1st Charm:

The first charm I know is unknown to rulers//or any of human kind// help it is named// for help it can give// in hours of sorrow and anguish.

#2 THURS

Thor and Giants, Twins and Duality, Self and Other

Alphabet letter #2 is B: Phoenician: 𐤁 Bēt – Hebrew: ב Bet.

Greek: Beta Β β.

The Phoenician letter Bet is derived from a hieroglyph that looks like a house.

In the Hebrew Alphabet Bet represents Mother Earth as a storehouse, or the concept of the goddess as a house. Marija Gimbutas excavated many statues of goddesses shaped like houses or vessels/containers.

In astrology Taurus (the second house) is followed by Gemini (the third house), marking a shift from a bull to twins. THURS is the rune of Thor and the giants (jǫtnar). Number two brings duality and "others".

In the Ogham the second letter represents the Rowan Tree (also known as the Quicken Tree). This got my attention because there are stories about Thor and the Rowan Tree.

> Earth was barren of and devoid of all plants when the goddess came down from Heaven and took the form of a Rowan Tree. After intercourse with the god of Thunder, the result was the creation of all the plants on Earth. *(Finnish creation myth)*[8]

Our metal mercury is linked to quicksilver, and used in making mirrors. It reflects the Self but also brings us face to face with the Double. Mercury is poisonous. It can deliver a "poison twin" or toxic double. I found many references to poison and toxicity here.

Once a piercing, wounding (or separation or conflict) occurs, healing and healers are needed. Healing is a long arduous journey, driven by the return to wholeness. To paraphrase the famous announcements here on London Underground: *mind the gap*! (And eventually close the gap).

Hávamál, 2nd Charm:

I know another //which all men need//who hope to be healers.

#3 ASS (áss in Old Norse)

The God Rune (Odin's rune)

Alphabet letter #3 is C. Phoenician: gīml (camel) 𐤂, Ancient Hebrew: Gimel ג .

Greek: Gamma (Γ γ).

This letter was derived from a hieroglyph depicting a weapon (either a staff sling or a spear thrower). We find weapons (and tools) at Rune KEN.

*Ansuz means *god*. Odin's name (the Old Norse spelling *Óðinn)* is derived from the Old Norse word O*ðr*: spirit, ecstasy, fury, frenzy, inspiration. Odin is also connected to the Old Norse word ǫnd: breath (as in the breath of life, the life-giving force).

Odin is the Allfather" (Old Norse *Alfaðir*). Snorri describes him as the "father of all gods". He is listed as the divine ancestor of royal families all over Northern Europe.[9]

Humans have an innate need to be of service. Human beings need an umbilical cord (or fetter) to spirit. This fetter is forged at ASS (ASS – KEN AXIS).

Hávamál, 3rd Charm:

I know a third// if I should need//to fetter any foe// it blunts the edge// of my enemy's sword// neither wiles nor weapons work.

#4 REID

Wagons, Riding and Journeys

Alphabet letter #4 is D. Phoenician letter #4 is Daleth (D) ◁, Hebrew: Dalet ד.

Greek Delta: (uppercase Δ, lowercase δ).

This letter was derived from an Egyptian Hieroglyph depicting a door (or fish).

The third position fetters (tethers) us to spirit or a God Force. However, the fourth position breaks or unravels bonds and sets us free, as time starts ticking and events start unfolding.

Rune REID may well have been derived from Ursa Major. Slavic traditions see the bears in the night sky as the hands of a cosmic clock.

Hávamál, 4th Charm:

I know a fourth// if I should find myself// fettered hand and foot// I shout the spell// that sets me free// bonds break from my feet// nothing holds my hands.

Job 38:31-32

Canst thou bind the sweet influences of Pleiades, or loose the bands of Orion? Canst thou bring forth Mazzaroth in his season? Or canst thou guide Arcturus with his sons?

#5 KEN

Tools and weapons, metallurgy and cosmetics

Alphabet letter #5 is E. Phoenician *hē* image 𐤄 .Hebrew He ה.

Greek: Epsilon (uppercase E, lowercase ε).

Derived from a hieroglyph depicting a window (and the next hieroglyph represents a weapon!)

Fascinating things happen at RUNE KEN, mirrored by alphabet stories from other locations. Blacksmiths start forging both tools and weapons. Teachers appear:

- In Scandinavia Freyja teaches women (and Odin) Seidr/ magical arts.
- In Greek mythology Prometheus steals (and gives people) fire.
- Azazel, the Leader of rebellious angels (in the book of Enoch), brings weapons and cosmetics. He also taught human beings about metallurgy and beautification.

> And Azazel taught men to make swords and knives and shields and breastplates; and made known to them the metals [of the earth] and the art of working them; and bracelets and ornaments; and the use of antimony and the beautifying of the eyelids; and all kinds of costly stones and all colouring tinctures.
>
> *-Book of Enoch 8:1–3a*

The next line is: *"And there arose much godlessness, and they committed fornication, and they were led astray and became corrupt in all their ways."* It points at the (shadow expression) of GIFU, and a Christian filter of morality.

In world myths an important teacher appears here and teaches human beings "forbidden skills from heaven". Tricksters appear too (our first glimpse of Loki).

KEN is a pine torch. The Anglo-Saxon futhorc has Rune CWEORTH, the fire stick.

In Norse mythology dwarfs are blacksmiths. KEN is the rune of arts, crafts and creativity. It is also the rune of tricksters and shamans (people who initiate others). Doing the bidding of the Norns turns Loki into a trickster (from a human perspective).

KEN brings danger and the risk of destruction. A pine torch can set things on fire. It also represents our inner fire (which produces light in the form of intellectual illumination). It can refer to physical eruptions (a boil or ulcer) and also emotions erupting like volcanoes. Illness can bring heat (fever).

In the rune sequence KEN follows REID. The constant "riding" is like rubbing, grinding, or polishing. It creates tracks. Under the surface of the established order, the primordial fire of Muspelheim continues to burn and crackle. The higher octave of this process is creativity: the forging of something new, a divine power. The lower octave is illness or weaponised relationships (armed conflict).

> Among the Yakut even the blacksmith who undertakes the ornamentation of the costume, must have inherited the right, 'If the blacksmith who makes a shamanistic ornament has not a sufficient number of ancestors, if he is not surrounded on all sides by the noise of hammering and the glow of fire, then birds with crooked claws and beaks will tear his heart in pieces.' For this reason, the blacksmith's vocation comes next in importance to the shaman's. In modern times it is practically impossible among the Yakut for the shaman's coat to be made, since there is now no class of hereditary blacksmiths.[10]

Learning and Law are both associated with number five. In Iceland the Law Court opened on the 5th day. Thursday was most holy day of the week in pre-Christian Scandinavia.

Hávamál, 5th charm:

I know a fifth// in battle's fury// if someone flings a spear// it speeds not so fast// but that I can stop it// I only have to see it.

#6 GIFU

Gift, sacred reciprocity, exchange, sacred marriage (sacrifice)

Letter #6 of the Alphabet is F. Phoenician Waw 𐤅 (Hook), Hebrew Vav: ו.

Both rune rows and alphabets evolved to meet the needs of changing times.

Originally the 6th letter of the Greek Alphabet was Wau or Digamma (uppercase: Ϝ, lowercase: ϝ) This letter disappears from the Greek ABC after Homer's time. Today letter #6 is Zeta (Ζ upper case, ζ lowercase).

This letter is derived from an Egyptian hieroglyph depicting a hook.

Rune Gifu is about gifts, exchange and sacred reciprocity. Odin says that every gift seeks or requires a return gift (the principle of reciprocity). At GIFU we also find the dark side of relationships and marriage: domestic violence and coercive control. Human encounters can lead to entanglements and unwelcome bonds.

Human sacrifices were made to Odin (especially by royal figures and enemy warriors). A spear or noose were used, mirroring the way Odin sacrificed himself to himself to acquire knowledge of the runes. His favour in battle was secured by throwing a spear over one's foes, sacrificing them to Odin with the cry, "Odin owns you all!" (Old Norse *Óðinn á yðr alla*).[11]

GIFU is also the rune of the Sacred Marriage. Proto-Indo Europeans had a tradition where the King married the Goddess of the Land. The regent was in service to land and divinity (not the other way around). A king who was sick, maimed or incapacitated was executed because they could no longer rule (their strength and virility reflected the state of the land).

An Arthurian legend tells us about the Fisher King, tasked with guarding the Holy Grail. He is both the protector and physical embodiment of his lands, but a wound (to his groin?) leaves him impotent and his kingdom barren.

In the epic Sumerian poem, the Descent of Inanna, King Dumuzi ploughs the goddess Inanna's Womb, her vulva.

In later myths we find references to mother goddesses losing authority to a king. The concept of the *hieros gamos* becomes distorted in patriarchal times. Some social commentators in the 2020s argue that the combination of birth control and dating apps (most notoriously Tinder) has taken this process of degradation to bottom rock level in our time.[12]

On the 6th day of Genesis God creates humanity. Friday is the day of Frigg and Freyja. It is also "marital date night": orthodox Jewish couples are expected to make love that night.

Hávamál, 6th Charm:

I know a sixth// if someone would harm me// by writing runes on a tree root// the man who wished// I would not come to woe// will meet misfortune, not I.

#7 Wynja

Frigg's rune: joy, pleasure, abundance, a "winning streak"

Alphabet letter is G. Phoenician 𐤆 (zayin) and Hebrew ז (zayin).

Greek: Eta – Eta (uppercase = H, lowercase = η).

This letter is derived from a hieroglyph depicting a weapon or manacle, one of two metal bands joined by a chain, for fastening a person's hands or ankles. (Some people use the word "shackled" for marriage).

When things go right, the sacred marriage between King and Land (Goddess) brings joy and prosperity to a thriving community.

Wynja is an old Germanic term denoting perfection, related to words still used in modern European languages: to wish (wunch in German, wens in Dutch), to win.

Hávamál, 7th Charm:

I know a seventh// if I see flames // high around a hall// no matter how far// the fire has spread// my spell can stop it.

#8 HAGAL

Hail, Hag, sudden cataclysmic events

Alphabet letter #8 is H.

Phoenician: Ḥet 𐤇 Hebrew Het ח (fence or gate).

The shape of the letter H harks back to the Egyptian hieroglyph for a courtyard (or wall, enclosure).

Greek: Theta, uppercase Θ and lowercase θ.

In all alphabets this letter (HAGAL included) looks like a gate. It opens the floodgates on a sudden destruction of the established order. It heralds either a symbolic death (initiation) or physical death. HAGAL also marks a fork in the road. A THURS-theme repeats here: HAGAL opens the duality of extreme outcomes: live or die, sink or swim etc. If we survive, such episodes lead to renewal or rebirth.

The Crossbar of Witch Rune Hagal

Our word *initiation* is derived from Latin. It literally means beginning, not ordeal. But initiation always involves the destruction of what is familiar and comfortable. Think of a construction made from Lego blocks: eventually this structure needs dismantling to free up building blocks for a new creation.

In all pantheons we meet a deity who embodies this principle. Saturn eats his own children. Kali wears a necklace of skulls. Skaði runs with wolves. Hecate is associated with crossroads.

Many rune magicians associate HAGAL with Heimdallr. His domain, Himinbjorg, is listed as the 8th hall of the gods in *Grímnismál*.

> Himinbjorg is the eight, and Heimdall there//O'er men hold sway, it is said;
> In his well-built house does the warder of heaven//The good mead gladly drink.
>
> *-Grímnismál, Poetic Edda*

The 8th house in astrology deals with death, inheritance, other people's money and regeneration through sexuality. Its ruler is the 8-legged Scorpion.

To me HAGAL is a gate to an enclosed medicinal garden (where poison plants grow alongside other medicinal plants). She is linked to the Elder Tree and an apothecary.

Hávamál, 8th charm:

I know an eighth// which no one on earth// could fail to find useful// when hatred waxes// among warriors// the spell will soothe them.

The Story of the First Aett of the UTHARK

The first Aett consists of the first eight runes. Let's tell their story:

At the very beginning of our current universe, the Primordial Cow Audhumbla (UR) suckles the primordial giant Ymir until both disappear. Audhumbla is probably dismembered along with Ymir. This is the sacrifice of the first giant (THURS). Ymir is the first being to die which, in the Vedas, makes him the Lord of the Land of the Dead (as Yama). His dismemberment sets the Wheel of Time (REID) in motion. Time runs, mysteriously and inexplicably (from a scientific point of view) forward, never backward.

The *Vǫluspá* speaks of three maidens present at the beginning of our world: the Norns (NAUD). They carve *ørlǫg* (primal law, the fate of all beings) and so the "Wheel of Karma" also starts turning because every action has an equal but opposite reaction (Newton's third Law of Motion). In plain English: karmic consequences.

> Thence come the maidens //mighty in wisdom,
> Three from the dwelling //down 'neath the tree//
> Urðr is one named// Verðandi the next//
> On the wood they scored //and Skuld the third.
> Laws they made there, and life allotted
> to the sons of men, and set their fates
> *-Vǫluspá st. 20*

UR is best conceptualized as a vast reservoir of cosmic energy, a womb-like Void, teeming with potential. This energy cannot be controlled, but it can be released or channelled, assigned a direction and velocity.

The *inverted horns* shape of rune UR resemble a cauldron. UR chimes with the name of the oldest Norn: Urðr. Her name is etymologically related to the Anglo-Saxon 12th century (time of Beowulf) word *wyrd* (which morphed into *weird* in modern English). It is also related to both *wort* (plant/herb) and *word*.

At Rune THURS both separation and primal wounding occurs, but *without the wound, there is no learning.* Learning has velocity (REID). The THURS-thorn pierces the bubble of Unity Consciousness (UR). It is the knife used to cut the umbilical cord.

A fork in the road appears. There is higher and lower octave of everything. Human beings exercise free will and develop a moral compass. The Birth of Time also brings Death in its wake, a sacred twin and foreshadowing of Rune EH.

In depth psychology the expulsion of birth starts a baby's journey of (eventually) experiencing oneself as separate from the mother. This process repeats in adolescence, when young people leave home.

No movement can occur until Duality (THURS) supplies two points two travel between. Divinity (ASS) breathes life into our spiritual journey: Self – God.

In the poem Vafþrúðnismál (*Poetic Edda*), Odin speaks to a dying dragon. Vafþrúðnir is a wise jǫtunn. His name comes from *Vaf,* which means weave or entangle, and *thrudnir,* which means strong or mighty (Mighty Entangler). At THURS we form entanglements with others.

Rune THURS is also Thor's hammer. Something has shattered or awakened, and this results in interaction between different realms. Things are unleashed: time, music and poetry flow.

At ASS the gods tether human beings to Divinity, before they embark on their epic journey. The divine gift of *free will* is granted. This involves an unbinding or uncoiling. An exodus of souls occurs.

The world of Time begins with penetration (a "thorn prick"). Time and Death enter the equation. This ancient knowledge lives on in the fairytale about Sleeping Beauty, where a literal, spiritual and sexual awakening occurs.

The Roman Goddess Juno was a midwife. Knots were forbidden in her worship because the presence of a knot could hinder delivery. This is the underlying principle of *knot magic:* making or untying knots or affects outcomes in the Web of Life. (At TYR the gods tie up the Fenris wolf).

Odin (ASS) is on a perpetual wisdom quest. Odin asks Freyja to teach him *seiðr*. Odin is mercurial, the Norse counterpart of Hermes. Hermes was a deity of trade and commerce, but also a trickster and God of Thieves. Odin steals the Mead of Poetry!

As Grímnir, the Masked One, he is the god with many faces. Once a split occurs between Self and Other, we become self-aware. We can choose to present different faces to the world, we can play and act. We can be either honest or deceptive.

At Rune ASS an ancient God utters/speaks/chants and impregnates, calling forth embryonic forms and beginnings. Time (REID) restricts and confines, it provides a container for our human experiences.

At UR the difference between Day and Night does not yet exist. It occurs when duality appears at THURS. The celestial bodies find their places in the heavens. Sun (SOL) and Moon map a circular path in the sky (the Zodiac).

Rune ASS is the Gift of Tongues and KEN is the Rune of Teachers. REID is the Turner of Time (Mundilfari).[13]

The Seventh Heaven on Earth is Frigg's realm (WYNJA). She wants joy and harmony for all beings.

Next, we meet the Dark Goddess at HAGAL. She howls like a wolf, rages and destroys. We perceive her as predatorial. Does she really have our best interests at heart?

HAGAL presents another Gateway. The Undivided "One God(dess)" offers no opening for returning spirits. Rune HAGAL forces us to undertake an epic underworld journey. The cosmic law of renewal demands dark nights of the soul.

AETT #2

Another journey or cycle-within-a-cycle starts here.

#9 Naud or Nyd

Alphabet letter #9 is I.

Phoenician ṭēt was derived from a hieroglyph depicting a wheel. ⨂

One variant is a circle with a dot or horizontal line inside (like the astrology symbol for the Sun).

⊙

Hebrew Tet ט

Greek Theta (uppercase Θ / lowercase θ) – Symbol of Death

IA The ninth letter of the Greek alphabet, iota (ιώτα) is written as I in uppercase and ι in lowercase.

NAUD is the rune of the Norns. The Phoenician wheel symbol could be perceived as the wheel of fortune and intersecting (or interacting with) individual threads of fate, called *ørlögþátto* in Old Norse. The Norns pull on the threads that connect us to other people and even non-humans (land, other species). Humans are interdependent beings. We all have threads of connection, cherishing some but neglecting or cutting others.

Our mortal coil, tethe or thread of life is cut by the Norns when we die.[14] Does it continue to uncoil in the other world as we join our Ancestors?

When we pass through the HAGAL Gateway, we survive *only if* the Norns carve this outcome. The Hag is linked to the Germanic figure of the *Hagadissa (also Haegtisse)*, who sat on the fence, which separated the village from the wilderness. She is the hedge rider, the herbalist, the healer.

Odin's 9th Charm in Hávamál:

I know a ninth// if I ever need// to save my ship in a storm// it will quiet the wind// and calm the waves// soothing the sea.

#10 IS

Ice, Icicle and Ice Bridge

Alphabet letter #10 is J.

Phoenician yōd: hand Ƶ. Hebrew: Yod י

Greek: Iota (ιώτα, uppercase I, lowercase ι)

Derived from a hieroglyph depicting an arm or hand, Yod is perceived as (God's) hand, arm or power in the Kabbalah.

Ice can act as a road or bridge. Time on ice brings visionary deep dreaming and clarity.

Bifrost is a rainbow by day and something else at night. I perceive it as an ice bridge, the road travelled by the souls of the dead. I link this bridge to the Milky Way. This icy celestial road forks near Scorpio.

The Galactic Centre is the rotational centre of the Milky Way. A river of stars flows between the territories of Orion-Gemini and Scorpio-Sagittarius. A fork in the road occurs near the Galactic Centre, the souls of the deceased face a choice.

The Vikings sailed in longships with dragonheads. They also buried people (of high standing) in boats. Were those otherworld ships intended to sail on a river of stars, perhaps to Noatun, the 11th Hall of the gods belonging to Njordr?

Winters were long and lethal in the Nordic region. Age was expressed as "how many winters a person had lived". Survival depended on a tight community (kith and kin, prioritising the collective over personal desires) and careful planning. The worst punishment was being an outcast, being outlawed.

In our day we have cryonics:

> Cryonics (from Greek: κρύος kryos meaning 'cold') is the low-temperature freezing (usually at −196 °C or −320.8 °F or 77.1 K) and storage of human remains, with the speculative hope that resurrection may be possible in the future.[15]

Hávamál, 10th Charm:

I know a tenth: Any time I see// witches sailing the sky// the spell I sing// sends them off their course; when they lose their skins// they fail to find their homes.

#11 JARA

The Harvest (of Souls)

(Etymologically related to Ger (harvest) and Ár (year).

Alphabet letter #11 is K.

Phoenician kāp 𐤊, Hebrew Kaf כ

Derived from a hieroglyph depicting the palm of a hand.

The scythe of the Grim Reaper brings food supplies.

A year is one crop cycle, also the interval between birthdays.

Hávamál, 11th Charm:

I know an eleventh// if I lead to war// good and faithful friends// under a shield I shout // the spell that speeds them/ well they fare in the fight// well they fare from the fight// wherever they go they fare well.

#12 Perthra

Rock or Dice Cup

Phoenician: lāmed 𐤋 image, letter: 𐤋, goad

Derived from a hieroglyph depicting a goad or cattle-prod, a farming tool used to spur and direct livestock, usually oxen pulling a cart or plough, or to round up cattle (FE).

Hebrew: Lamed ל (related to acquiring knowledge).

Greek: Lambda (uppercase Λ, lowercase λ).

PERTHRA is the rune of rocks and mountains and caves. Some ancient graves were womb-shaped. Both kings and poets sat out on burial mounds to commune with the dead.

In Scandinavia we find many grave mounds. Marking graves with a cross was a later (Christian) practice. Perthra hints at the continuation of consciousness after death.

> *Temples and tombs were built in the likeness of the Mother of the Dead or Mother Earth's pregnant belly or womb; this is the key to understanding megalithic structures and their floor plans. The idea that caves and caverns are natural manifestations of the primordial womb of the goddess is not Neolithic in origin; it goes back to the Palaeolithic, when a cave's narrow passages, oval-shaped areas, clefts, and small cavities were marked or painted entirely in red, a colour that must have symbolized the colour of the mother's generative organs.*[16]

In astrology the 12th House belongs to watery Pisces. Traditionally its ruler is Jupiter, who takes 12 years to spin around the Zodiac.

Hávamál, 12th Charm:

I know a twelfth// if up in a tree// I see a corpse hanging high// the mighty runes// I write and colour// make the man come down// to talk with me.

HALFWAY INTERLUDE

Rune #12

(PERTHRA in the Uthark) marks the half-way point on the Wheel

There are 24 runes, so position #12 marks the halfway point. In the Uthark this is PERTHRA and the next rune EOH sits directly opposite UR.

The space between #12 and #13 holds magical power and is comparable to *Vargtimmen*: The Wolf Hour. This is the hour between night and dawn, when most people die. Sleep is deepest (so a good time for burglars too!) and nightmares are most vivid. This is the hour when insomniacs feel haunted, ghosts visit, and most babies are born.

The guardian of this halfway space is the Fenris Wolf: son of trickster god Loki. He does the bidding of the Norns and will play a key role in Ragnarök.

The period of Twelfth Night (also known as the Twelve Nights of Christmas, stretching to Epiphany) is a liminal time of year and not without risks.[17] *Saturnalia* was an ancient Roman festival celebrated in the 12th month. Briefly the world turned upside down in sacred role reversal: the masters served the slaves. Medieval Europe had the tradition of the Boy Bishop where a boy was chosen (often a chorister) to parody the adult bishop (commonly on the feast of the Holy Innocents, on 28 December). Something "goes upside down" or "belly up" at position #12.

This space makes or breaks us. We grow our spine and find our courage. Our spinal column has 24 vertebrae.

Significations of Pisces are: completion, visions and addictions, alcohol (the word *spirits* has two meanings, disincarnate beings and strong alcoholic drinks). Things can go "both ways" at position 12

#13 EOH

World Tree and Axis

Alphabet letter 13 is M. Phoenician: mēm 𐤌 Hebrew: mem מ and ם (mem sofit). *In Greek it is Nu: uppercase N, lowercase ν.*

Mem is believed to derive from the Egyptian hieroglyphic symbol for water (the rune equivalent is LAGU).

Some cultures view the Placenta as either our Twin or our Ancestor in the Womb. This "personal tree" keeps us nourished, tethered and alive.

Eoh is the axis mundi or rotational axis.

Yew is intensely toxic and planted in graveyard. Yew's fumes are hallucinogenic, and its wood was used for making lethal long bows. (EH)

Hávamál, 13th Charm:

I know a thirteenth// if I pour water// over a youth// he will not fall// in any fight// swords will not slay him.

Letter #14 ALGIZ

Moose, Elk Sedge, Antlered or Horned Being

(Poetic licence: crow's foot, swan in flight, animal rune)

Alphabet letter #14 is N. Phoenician: nūn 𐤍, Hebrew: nun (serpent or fish). In Greek it is Xi: uppercase Ξ, lowercase ξ; Greek: ξι.

Dillon observes that the Phoenician letter Nun (serpent-fish) is written with the shape of Draco, defeated ruler of the North Stars.

Greek: mu (μυ) is written as M in uppercase and μ in lowercase.

The fourteenth letter of the Arabic alphabet, Nun, is equivalent to the Hebrew or Phoenician nun. The letter in all three alphabets is derived from a pictogram of a fish or serpent. In Arabic: Nun means Leviathan.

Rune poems link ALGIZ to Elk Sedge. Our word Elk derives from the Latin ALCIS, the name of an ancient Germanic (twin) god. The word *Älg* in Swedish is habitually translated by Scandinavian authors as elk, but Swedish "elks" are moose! These words unfailingly cause confusion in any rune class containing participants from both Europe and the Americas!

At ALGIZ we encounter the Wild God or Wild One, a representative of the animal kingdom. We evaluate our connection to Nature – and our own nature

Horned gods bring protection and fertility to land. The demonization that occurs at THURS intensifies at ALGIZ (both runes are used in protection workings and sigils.) Christianity turns ancient gods into horned "devils" with goat's hooves.

> According to folklore Sami god Leib-olmai, ("Alder Man") is a forest deity who and guardian of wild animals, especially bears (echoes of Finnish god Tapio). Hunters made offerings of small bows and arrows to Leib-olmai to ensure success in the chase. Leib means "blood," and

> the red juice from alder bark, symbolizing blood, was splattered over the hunters as they returned with a dead bear.[18]

ALGIZ represents the spirit worker (clad in ceremonial garments, merged with animal spirits). My research also shows associations with the Horned Serpent, found in the night sky and under the roots of the world tree.

Our modern peace symbol shows an upside down ALGIZ rune inside a circle.

Odin's 14th Charm in Hávamál:

I know a fourteenth// as men will find// when I tell them the tales of the gods// I know all about// the elves and the Æsir// few fools can say as much.

INTERLUDE: A REFLECTION ON (HORNED) SERPENTS

The dragon *Níðhǫggr* gnaws at one root of Yggdrasil, stretching over Niflheim. He also chews on the corpses of "low-lives" (those guilty of murder, adultery, and oath-breaking, which Norse society considered some of the worst possible crimes) at Nástrǫnd. The squirrel Ratatoskr runs between the eagle at the top of the tree and the serpent-dragon below and passes messages.

World serpent Jormungandr (also *Miðgarðsormr or Midgard Serpent* in Old Norse) is often perceived as destructive too (locked in constant battle of wills with Thor) but this serpent binds our world together, a vital task.

The Elder Futhark does not have a serpent rune, but the Anglo-Saxon Futhorc has Rune IOR (aquatic animal/serpent). Serpents are notorious for producing venom. In the Bible a serpent tempts Adam and Eve to eat from the Tree of Knowledge.

I glimpse serpents at THURS (toxicity) and at BJARKA (poison as medicine).

The poem *Gylfaginning* says that one sign of Ragnarok being imminent is the violent unrest of the sea, as Jǫrmungandr releases its tail from its mouth. Land will flood and the serpent will thrash on the shore. Jörmungandr will advance, spraying poison to fill the air and water, beside Fenrir, whose eyes and nostrils blaze with fire (and whose monstrous jaws touch both earth and the sky). The prediction is that Thor will kill Jǫrmungandr but drop dead after walking nine paces, due to the serpent's deadly venom.

After 3000 BCE Draco (the celestial dragon) lost his position as the ruler of the Pole star (axial precession). Stories about St George "slaying a dragon" may link to precession. Ancient bull gods once assumed the form of serpents. They possessed the mercurial quality of shapeshifting.[19]

Eve and Adam are expelled from Paradise after eating fruit from the Tree of Knowledge. They enter the Earth realm of time restrictions, making choices, loss and grief. (I interpret the fall from paradise as the locus of Unity Consciousness).

Letter #15 SOL

Sunna, the Sun

Alphabet letter #15 is O. Phoenician sāmek 𐤎 Hebrew Samekh ס

Greek Xi: Ξ ξ

Derived from a hieroglyph depicting a pillar (*axis mundi?*)

At SOL the Sun returns and there is light at the end of the tunnel. We have been initiated. We nearly died. We have had time on ice and needed cave time (PERTHRA) to lick our wounds. Now we need to grow antlers and reclaim our feral selves (ALGIZ). SOL is the moment of sunrise in our spiritual lives. We return to the world as a changed person.

Norse cosmology views the Sun as a giantess travelling across the sky in a chariot drawn by two horses. Those horses point forward to Rune EH.

Hávamál, 15th Charm:

I know a fifteenth // that first Thjodrerir // Sang before Delling's doors//Giving power to gods//prowess to elves// Fore-sight to Hroptatyr Odin. [*Delling's Doors* means Dawn.]

Letter #16 TYR

Spiritual warrior, sacrifice for collective good

Alphabet letter is O. Phoenician: Ayin (Eye) written as a circle with a dot in the middle.

Hebrew: Ayin/Eye, written as ע. It has the same name and origin as the Phoenician letter, but it looks different. It does not have a sound of its own, but it can indicate a vowel or a glottal stop.[20]

Greek: Pi (Π, π)

Tyr is the spiritual warrior god. Here face our inner warrior, our moral compass and our willingness to make sacrifices to safeguard those we love, or the values we embody.

Hávamál, 16th Charm:

For the sixteenth I know// if a modest maiden's favour and affection I desire to possess// the soul I change of the white-armed damsel// and wholly turn her mind.[21]

The Story of the Second Aett

Aett #2 NAUD IS JARA PERTHRA EOH ALGIZ SOL TYR

The Norns (NAUD) show their hand after HAGAL brings devastation. We tighten our belt and *do the necessary*. We build character and develop self-discipline. Time on ice (IS) means serious contemplation of a new direction in life. When we live from our chiselled new self, things come full circle. We flower and bear fruit.

Some perceive PERTHRA as the dice cup used by Vikings in their games. This metaphor shows a container or cosmic womb, where potentialities rattle around until they flip into definite outcomes. We call that process *Fate*. The patterning of those dice is decided by the Norns.

Some say that mathematics, in its abstract purity, is the primordial language of the universe but I believe that *patterning* is the primordial language of the universe. Mythology is just one medium showing this patterning (our own body is another). So are star constellations.

As above so below
As within so without
As the universe, so the soul
-Attributed to Hermes Trismegistus

Human beings are not spineless. We work out what our personal world evolves around (EOH). We set priorities. In this process we become like a tree: we shelter and protect our children or mentees under the canopy. We grow roots and we reach for the stars. We raise dreamers and visionaries, architects of a future we ourselves will not witness.

At ALGIZ we encounter a Wild God and evaluate our connection to Nature – and our own nature.

At THURS demonisation (fear of the Other or Outsider) occurs and this theme intensifies at ALGIZ. Between SOL and TYR a warrior dies in battle or is reborn with the *Sol Invictus* (Unconquered Sun).

#17 BJARKA

Birch, Healer, Mother

Alphabet letter #17 is Q. Phoenician: pē 𐤐 (derived from a hieroglyph depicting a mouth).

Hebrew: PE (mouth or commandment), ף פ פּ

Greek: Rho Ρρ (phonetic value R)

This is the rune of the birch tree and of women's mysteries and rituals in Slavic culture. Women still birth all human beings until today; artificial wombs do not (yet) exist. From dust we come and to dust we return but our mother's body turns star dust into *us*: living breathing people (MADR).

During gestation we float in amniotic fluid. The waters break and we ride into the world on our personal wave. Those waters protected us and kept us alive (LAGU).

When a mother offers her body as a sacred space, her womb becomes the human embodiment of the cosmic womb.

Biargrunar are Birth Runes, pointing at the sacred office of a midwife.

Hávamál, 17th charm:

For the seventeenth I know// that the young maiden will reluctantly avoid me. These songs, Loddfafnir// thou wilt long have lacked// yet it may be good if thou understandest them// profitable if thou learnest them.

#18 EH

Horse Rune, Sleipnir's Rune, Twins and Partnerships. Psycho Pomp or Soul Conductor

Alphabet letter #18 is R. Phoenician: Ṣādē ٣, ٣ letter ٣, derived from a hieroglyph depicting a papyru plant or fish hook.

Hebrew Ṣādi or Tzadik ץ צ צ

Greek: Σ σ/ς

Duality spirals around again!

This is the rune of 8-legged horse Sleipnir and of Death. At EH we either live in fear of Death or we learn to safely navigate other worlds long before we die. We need partners and soul mates along that challenging journey. That is why Death is also the rune of twins and partnership.

Between this rune and the next we travel from EH to MADR: In the moment of Death, we join our Ancestors; we become an Ancestor ourselves. A human rider merges with a horse psychopomp, in Bronze Age petroglyphs?

Hávamál, 18th Charm:

For the eighteenth I know// that which I never teach to maid or wife of man// all is better what one only knows// this is the closing of the songs//save her alone who clasps me in her arms or is my sister.

#19 MADR

Human being, mankind, ancestors

Alphabet letter #19 is S. Phoenician: Qōp, Φ Hebrew: Qof ק

Greek: Phi, Φφ

Derived from a hieroglyph depicting the eye of a needle.

This is the rune of human beings in every possible sense: personhood, generations, ancestors and descendants; also, of the human condition and human-centred thinking.

Our word man derives from the root-stem Manu (also found in MADR). It's Indo-European and comes to us from Sanskrit.[22] The word has the following meanings: archetypal man, first man or progenitor of humanity. The Sanskrit term for human (mānava) really means "from Manu", or "the children of Manu". In later texts, Manu is the title or name of fourteen mystical rulers of earth. They appear at the beginning of each cyclical aeon, when the universe is born anew.

There is no 19th charm in Hávamál but the poem Loddfáfnismál closes with:

Now are sung the High One's songs, in the High One's Hall, to the sons of men all-useful, but useless to the sons of jǫtnar (ON one jǫtunn, several jǫtnar). Hail to him who has sung them!

Hail to him who knows them! May he profit who has learnt them! Hail to those who have listened to them!

#20 LAGU

Water, by extension emotions and flow, lunar cycles

Alphabet letter #20 is T. Phoenician: Res, Hebrew: Resh.

Greek: upsilon, Y υ

Derived from a hieroglyph showing a mouth.

Lagu refers to all bodies of water: the sea, lakes and rivers; also, blood and bodily fluids, "our inner ocean". Many things are associated with the Moon. We find them all at LAGU.

In creation stories from different continents a deluge destroys our world, and a new world comes into being. Water supports life and kills. Water is both amniotic fluids, used in baptism, yet wipes out entire communities with tsunamis. It provides fish (food) but harbours sharks. The astrology symbol for Pisces shows two fishes swimming in opposite directions.

After the deluge a Hero must carry knowledge and wisdom to safety, to preserve it for future generations. In the Bible this is Noah, but in the Elder Futhark this is Tyr.

The Hag is pregnant with a "Messianic Fish": Ichtus (ἰχθύς), adopted by early Christians as a secret symbol. Jesus, the Messiah, famously feeds 5,000 people, the hungry multitude, on just five loaves of bread and two fish.

Rune LAGU has also been linked to leeks. *Laguz or *Laukaz is the reconstructed Proto-Germanic name of this rune.[23]

In *Vǫlsa þáttr:*

> The old woman stood up, approached her son, and took the thing [horse penis] from him, saying there was no

need to waste a thing which might be of use. She then went into the kitchen, dried the member carefully, and wrapped it in a linen cloth along with leeks and other herbs, to prevent it from rotting, and then laid it into her coffer...

All that autumn she would retrieve it every evening and address it with a prayer of worship, believing it to be her god, and making the rest of the household accept this heresy. By the power of the devil the thing grew and became so strong, that it could stand upright by the old woman, when she wanted it to.[24]

If I command the moon, it will come down; and if I wish to withhold the day, night will linger over my head; and again, if I wish to embark on the sea, I need no ship, and if I wish to fly through the air, I am free from my weight.

-Thessalian Witches[25]

#21 ING

Seed, storehouse of potential, reproduction and sexuality.

Alphabet letter #21 is W. Phoenician: sin or shin, W Hebrew: šīn ש.

From a hieroglyph depicting a tooth (or the sun).

Historically Sin gave rise to the Greek Sigma (Σ) (which in turn gave Latin S and Cyrillic C), and the letter *Sha* in the Glagolitic and Cyrillic scripts (ш, Ш).

Greek: Φ φ

Yngvi is an older name for fertility god Freyr. ING is a seed, a storehouse teeming with potential. It requires careful planting and tending. It is also the rune of reproduction (both sexual and non-sexual). At EH we confront our death. At ING we reflect on our legacy and tend our offspring.

#22 ODAL

(Ancestral) Home, Enclosure or Sanctuary, Homeland, Place of Belonging

(Swaps places with DAGAZ in an alternative sequence)

Alphabet letter #22 is V.

Phoenician: Taw or Tav. Hebrew: Tav,תָּו, the final letter of these alphabets.

From a hieroglyph depicting a mark.

Greek continues up to 24 letters, ending with Omega, a container, womb or "uterus-shaped homeland".

Greek: Chi, X χ, which looks like a cross. In Plato's *Timaeus* (c. 360 BC) it is explained that the two bands that form the soul of the world cross each other like the letter X (Rune GIFU but it also makes me think of the two "celestial belts" of the ecliptic and the Zodiac).[26]

> My Father's house has many rooms; if that were not so, would I have told you that I am going there to prepare a place for you? 3 And if I go and prepare a place for you, I will come back and take you to be with me that you also may be where I am.
>
> *John 14:2-3 New International Version (NIV)*

At ODAL is our home and sanctuary and knowing where we belong.

Many people struggle with questions about lineage and belonging: *where is home?* That is the ultimate ODAL question (or quest). As is the question: does consciousness continue after death? Do I have a "soul home" in eternity?

#23 DAGAZ

Light, Illumination, Enlightenment, Higher Perspective

Alphabet letter #23 is W.

This letter has no Phoenician or Hebrew equivalent.

Greek: Psi, Ψ ψ

If we arrange the Egyptian hieroglyphs according to phonetic values (so the ABC sequence applies), the final letter represents a sleeping serpent. This mimics India's Black Goddess, which resides at the base of each human spine. Awakening of kundalini leads to enlightenment. She will ascend along the 24 vertebrae of the "spine tree" until she emerges from the Crown.[27]

The twin gates of Duality opened at THURS and they close again at DAGAZ. We have arrived at a higher perspective, bridging contradiction. THURS – DAGAZ is the axis of the dialectic process.

The halls of the Norse gods are primordial expressions of ODAL, divine homesteads in other realms. If we take this concept one step further, DAGAZ represents the three mysterious Norse realms of Immortality, where the Light Elves live.

DAGAZ is also about Light as a metaphor for the Divine.

#24 FE

(Letter #24 FE in the Uthark but #1 in the Futhark)

Domesticated cattle, mobile wealth, fee, money

Greek: Omega, Ω ω

Ogham ends with YEW, a poisonous tree planted in graveyards.

By FE we are in the Neolithic period. The earlier hunter-gatherers have settled are now keeping livestock and growing crops.

Money was intended a neutral means for trading and exchange but became force driving greed.

The Viking had drinking horns, used in their halls (ODAL) to drink mead (ASS – LAGU) and welcome home the warriors (TYR). FE is a rune of achievement and completion.

Story of the Third Aett

The Universal Journey and astronomical principles.

BJARKA – EH – MADR – LAGU – ING – ODAL – DAGAZ – FE

The third A*ett* starts with BJARKA, a pioneer tree.

Between TYR and BJARKA we move from the masculine principle of justice and order, (qualities expected in a good *Pater Familias),* to the healing/nurturing and death-tending qualities of the Mother. Together these two runes offer the higher octave of sacred masculine and divine feminine energies.

In the Third Aett we meet Death (EH) as the end of physical life.

Our word *matter* is closely related to the Latin word *mater* (mother). Incarnation is spirit made flesh. The return journey is death. Every mother goddess is also a death goddess, by necessity (BJARKA – NAUD). The Cosmic MOTHER brings the souls of her children home again, to her cosmic womb.

Hindu goddess Kali is one famous manifestation of the Pregnant Hag. Also called Kali Mata, she is the Dark Mother, associated with Death, sexuality and violence. She wears a necklace of decapitated heads or skulls. (Compare this to Brisingamen, Freyja's Necklace!)[28]

At the End of Time (Ragnarok) she will take the seed (ING) of her spouse Shiva (blended with ashes from the cremation ground) into herself and bring forth another universe. The Galactic Center, located in Sagittarius, is the rotational axis of the Milky Way galaxy. On a mystical level it is the cosmic womb.

Kali resides in close proximity to cremation grounds where all elements interact and earthly attachments are dissolved: this is the cosmic Cycle of Life – Death – Rebirth. Sir John Woodroffe wrote that "Kali is so called because She devours Kala (Time) and then resumes Her own dark formlessness." REID has been devoured. We are back at UR, which contains ING (the seed of a new universe).[29]

Human beings (MADR) experience joy and grief (LAGU) and form partnerships (EH). Some become soul conductors long before they die.

LAGU is the place where the Moon shines on water and pulls on the tides of our emotions. After a sea change or deluge a Hero (TYR) must carry ancestral wisdom to safety, to preserve it as a seedpod (ING) for future generations.

FE is the rune of a settled and prosperous civilization (and eventually of capitalism) but an aurochs with massive horns appears on the horizon. Chaos makes its presence felt. Heimdallr stands ready to blow the gjallarhorn. The Old Norse word Ragnarok has become a term used in common speech.

Chapter 9

Stjörnuíþrótt: Old Norse Astronomy

> *Mythology is often a metaphorical way of looking at natural phenomena; in older cultures, myth plays the role later acted by science.*
>
> *-Dr. Karl E. H. Seigfried*[1]

Once day I worked up to midnight in my Forest Studio in Sweden. I stepped out of the building and was greeted by a dazzling night sky (there is no light pollution because there are no other houses in the vicinity). I suddenly saw all the runes in the night sky over my head and thought: were the runes inspired by star constellations?

"Star Oddi"

In the 12th century a man called Star Oddi (*Stjörnu-Oddi* in Icelandic) worked as a farm labourer in northern Island. His proper name was Oddi Helgason. He made careful observations and achieved remarkable knowledge for his time. He wrote down the position of the Sun for every day in his location, and calculated the dates of the summer and winter solstices. His work gave the sea-faring Vikings a useful source of orientation for sea-faring. Research shows that the Vikings may have navigated the open seas using sunstones, naturally occurring crystals that filter polarized light.[2]

Oddi produced one piece of writing: *Oddatala* (Oddi's Tale). It is only a few pages long and divided into three chapters. The text covers the exact time and date of solstices, in the context of leap years. The second chapter specified the position of the Sun over a year. The last chapter describes the direction of dawn and nightfall, through the year. His observations made a significant contribution to the Julian calendar, introduced in his time. It reformed the Roman calendar, (which was designed with input from Greek mathematicians and Greek astronomers), but required corrections and adjustments. Over large periods of time inaccuracies creep in due to Axial Precession. Oddi's observations surpassed Christian data.

Over extremely long periods of time our familiar star patterns (Orion, Ursa Major, Ursa Minor etc.) will stretch and change shape.[3] This is because of a phenomenon called *proper motion*. Astronomers define this as a gradual change in the position of a star or other object on the celestial sphere, which is the result of the object's intrinsic motion through space rather than its apparent motion as observed from Earth. Let's enjoy what we see today.

Mythology versus Cosmology

I prefer the word *cosmology* to the word *mythology,* because it refers to a coherent belief system, often aligned with a particular location and ancestral tradition. A cosmology offers a cognitive map for understanding and navigating both this world and other realms.

Human beings have always tried to make sense of their surroundings and the Cosmos, using all means available to them.

Myth is a peculiar word because it contains opposite meanings: *a traditional story about a timeless (metaphoric) truth* and *a widely held but false belief or idea* (falsehood or fiction).

The opening poem of the *Poetic Edda,* the *Völuspá* (Prophecy of the Seeress), tells of a time before the world was made:

> *There was no sand nor sea nor chill waves, no earth to be found*
> *nor high heaven, a gulf of gaping void, and grass was nowhere.*

The Sanskrit *Nāsadīya Sūkta,* the creation hymn, opens in a remarkably similar fashion:

There was neither non-existence nor existence, no realm of air nor sky beyond... There was no death then, nor immortality, there was no sign of night nor of day.[4]

Before Northern Europe was converted to Christianity, the Eddic poems and myths helped Norse people understand the world, and their own place in the world. The Old Norse people developed a unique cosmology, which contains traces from an earlier period (of Indo-European migration). The Vedas are a collection of hymns and other religious texts written (in Vedic Sanskrit) in India between about 1500 and 1000 BCE.

Today it has become fashionable to pull stories out of their historical context (essentially turning them into ships without an anchor) for our own purposes. We can only understand myths if we study the culture that produced them. This painstaking process involves stripping ourselves of the blinkers and filters of perception, which belong to our own era.

Please read this chapter with the *Stellarium app* open (on your phone or tablet), set to the Norse night sky. On a bright starry night, visit a place with the lowest light pollution that your surroundings and circumstances allow. Look up or even lie down (to make it easier to see the starry dome). Bring binoculars if you can. Allow yourself to see a completely different (ancient, ancestral) cosmology overhead. This chapter invites ancestral time travel!

Star Patterns

We have no written record of astronomy practiced by the ancient peoples of Northern Europe. What we know is limited but tantalising. We know for sure that they did not perceive the same constellations we see today. They joined up the stars in a different way.[5]

The familiar Western constellations come to us from ancient Babylonian and Sumerian astronomers. Arabian astronomers brought them to Egypt from Crete (after a volcanic eruption). From Egypt this knowledge travelled onto Rome and spread all over Europe.

In 150 AD a Greek scientist called Ptolemy published a book titled the *Almagest*, describing 1,022 stars and names 48 constellations. The constellations of the Zodiac are some of the oldest recorded. Essentially, they have not changed since Babylonian astronomers recorded them in the 6th century B.C.E.

This chapter even includes some material from the Nordic Bronze Age (c. 2000/1750 – 500 BC), long before the Viking Era.

For many centuries people have added to our knowledge base. When navigators rounded the Horn of Africa they observed unknown new stars, which can only be seen from the Southern Hemisphere.[6]

In 1922 the International Astronomical Union codified the sky into the 88 official constellations used by the Western World today and defined their boundaries (there was overlap and confusion before). This is not about drawing a beautiful picture, but it places every star and celestial object inside the boundaries of a constellation. Everything has its proper place and can be found there, celestial housekeeping.[7]

We do have a body of written source material that makes up the cosmology and mythology of Scandinavia. Those poems and myths were written down in 13th century Iceland (two centuries after the Christianisation of the Nordic region).

However, there is not one coherent or seamless mythology of Scandinavia. This is a diverse collection of material sourced from a large geographical region. It is likely that (key elements of) some myths originate in the Iron Age. Stories and myths are living things: they are forever shifting morphing, being re-told by a new generation of skalds or bards to serve a new purpose etc. There is not 'one historically true version' of such myths, but we are fortunate to have some versions frozen in time.

What We Know for Sure

At the heart of Norse cosmology is a world tree: Yggdrasil. Said to be either an ash or a yew, it is also a cognitive map and tool.

> There is an eagle that sits in the branches of the ash, and it has knowledge of many things, and between its eyes sits a hawk called Vedrfolnir. A squirrel called Ratatosk runs up and down through the ash and carries malicious messages between the eagle and Nidhogg. Four stags run in the branches of the ash and feed on the foliage. Their names are: Dain, Dvalin, Dunyr, Durathror.[8]

The Finnish epic, the *Kalavala,* describes a similar tree:

> At that old *Väinämöinen* sings and practices his craft: He sang a spruce topped with flowers topped with flowers and leaved with gold; the top he pushed heavenward through the clouds he lifted it spread the foliage skyward across heaven scattered it. He sings, practices his craft– sang the moon to gleam on the gold-topped spruce, he sang the Great Bear on to its boughs.[9]

Millstone Model of the Cosmos

Nigel Pennick writes about the symbolism of the mill stone. Traditionally a connection was made between women using a spinning wheel or distaff and the Norns conceptualised as spinning the threads of life and weaving the Web of Wyrd.

Medieval law banned women with spindles and distaffs from going near mills because the large circular stones (which grind flour in a mill) can be understood as a metaphor of the cosmos. The sky is viewed as rotating above a fixed earth, where the upper mill stone turns on the lower one (our world). The lower stone has a hole in the middle which allows the axletree to rotate. The oldest (and simplest) form of water mill reflected a tripartite cosmos: the waters of the underworld (circled by the world serpent), the fixed earth (our world or Midgard, the lower millstone) and the rotating upper stone (the heavens and night sky).

In Snorri Sturluson's Eddic poem Skáldskaparmál, Snaebjorn tells of nine skerry maidens turning a mill: *Amlóða kvern* (Amlóði's Quern, also Hamlet's Mill) is a kenning for the sea being cut or churned by the prow of a ship. It so becomes part of a celestial mill 'grinding the meal of the strewn stars.'[10]

Stjǫrnuíþrótt

The Old Norse word for astronomy is *Stjǫrnuíþrótt:* the science of the observation of the stars.[11] The Old Norse people excelled at this skill. They lived near (some even North of) the Arctic Circle, where the Sun remains below the horizon around the winter solstice. Spending 24 hours a day in total darkness made people pay close attention to the stars.

Astronomy can be used for determining both the time of day and a location. This makes it useful for both agricultural purposes and navigation. Many Norse poems were linguistic masterpieces, (apparently) designed to aid memorization. Old Norse culture was pre-literate, or illiterate, and people had a strong oral tradition of memorizing and reciting poems (bundled together in the Eddas).

The Voluspa describes how the 'firmament" was made from Ymir's skull to support the stars (sparks from Muspelheim). Four dwarves hold up Ymir's' skull. They are named for the directions of the compass.

Encrypted astronomical information has been found in the Norse myths. There are astronomically significant numbers recorded in the Edda:

23. Five hundred doors and forty there are,
I ween, in Valhall's walls;
Eight hundred fighters through one door fare
When to war with the wolf they go.[12]

The number 540 has the factors 20, a standard numerical unit known as *a score*, and 27, which is the number of the *sidereal lunar cycle* (the number of days it takes for the moon to return to the same place in the sky). When you multiply 540 and 800 it makes 432,000 which is astronomically important.

The Eddic poem Grímnismál contains a fascinating description of the Norse cosmology and the domains of the gods. It references the astronomically significant number 432. However, an earlier portion of the poem describing the domains of the gods has a distinct *sexagesimal* (a numerical system with 60 as its base, think of our clock.) influence because *twelve* homes of the gods and goddesses are described:

1 *Thrudheim (ON* Þrúðheimr) *for Thor as well as Ydalir* (the yewdales apparently in Thrudheim) for Ull who is his stepson
2 *Alfheim* (ON Álfheimr) *for Frey*
3 *Valaskjálf* for Vali
4 *Sǫkkvabekkr* for Saga (who may or may not be Frigg)
5 *Gladsheim* (ON Glaðsheimr) *for Odin which has within it Odin's hall – Valhalla*
6 *Thrymheim* (ON Þrymheimr) *for the giantess Skadi who rules it after her father Thiazi dies*
7 *Breidablik* (ON Breiðablik) *for Balder*
8 *Himinbjorg for Heimdal*
9 *Folkvang* (ON Fólkvangr) *for Freya*
10 *Glitnir for Forseti*
11 *Noatun (ON* Nóatún*) for Njord*
12 *Landvidi* (Landvíði) *for Vidar*

Is it a coincidence that the Zodiac has, for thousands of years, been divided into twelve segments or houses? Do ancient Mesopotamian numbers appear in a Norse poem? Freya Aswynn pioneered the idea of the domains (or palaces) of twelve gods as the houses of the Zodiac.[13]

Alvíssmál

There are direct references to heavenly bodies in Norse Mythology. The poem Alvíssmál clearly demonstrates that the people who wrote the myths had knowledge of the sky and celestial bodies. It contains a series of back-and-forth questions and answers about what the heavenly bodies are called by various tribes or nations. Thor asks Alvis (All Wise) these questions to test the knowledge of the dwarf, who is after his daughter Trud.[14]

We learn that what humans call Earth is:

> 10. " 'Earth' to men, 'Field' | to the gods it is,
> 'The Ways' is it called by the Wanes;
> 'Ever Green' by the giants, | 'The Grower' by elves,
> 'The Moist' by the holy ones high."

Heaven is:

> 12. " 'Heaven' men call it, | 'The Height' the gods,
> The Wanes 'The Weaver of Winds';
> Giants 'The Up-World,' | elves 'The Fair-Roof,'
> The dwarfs 'The Dripping Hall.'"

The Moon (Máni)

> 14. Moon' with men, 'Flame' | the gods among,
> 'The Wheel' in the house of hell;

'The Goer' the giants, | 'The Gleamer' the dwarfs,
The elves 'The Teller of Time.

The Sun (Sól or Sunna)

16. "Men call it 'Sun,' | gods 'Orb of the Sun,'
'The Deceiver of Dvalin' the dwarfs;
The giants 'The Ever-Bright,' | elves 'Fair Wheel,'
'All-Glowing' the sons of the gods."

(Like trolls) dwarfs turn to stone if they are exposed to sunlight, so they are familiar with the Moon.

Scholars of cultural astronomy (the combined fields of *archeoastronomy* and *ethnoastronomy)* have suggested that the timeless global collection of stories we call *world myths*, are (ultimately) astronomical in origin. The stories about deities and creator beings are based on the movements of planetary bodies and other celestial objects.

My Own Questions

Are there any astronomical runes?
Are all runes (possibly) astronomical runes?

The longer I work with Rune REID, the more I perceive it as the rune of Cosmic Cycles, as it is the rune of *all things coming full circle*. It contains all stories, even those of Mythic Time (or Deep Time, before human memory existed).

Rune TYR is obviously astronomical due to axial precession. Over very long periods the pole star loses its prominence (right position) and another star takes over. This phenomenon is caused by the axis of our planet shifting.

> Precession is the periodic wobble of the earth, which spins like a spinning top. When the Earth wobbles, it does it over a very long period of time and the wobble only makes one complete revolution every 25,920 years. This figure divided by the sexagesimal base number 60 results in *the significant number* 432. There is further evidence that the ancient Norse divided up the heavens into equal slices of a 360 circular pie, echoing the approach of the Babylonians and Sumerians with their use of sexagesimal calculations, just like we currently use sexagesimal instruments such as the watch and clock, along-side standard decimal mathematics.[15]

In Neolithic times *alpha draconis* was the Pole Star. At the beginning of the Common Era, it was the lode star *32 Camelopardi*. The present Pole Star, *Polaris Alpha Ursae Minoris*, also known as the Nail or Nowl, attained its present status as the Pole Star around the year 1400. It is also known as Tir, Tyr's star. For over 2,000 years, Polaris has aligned above the North Pole, aiding navigators. However, after CE 2100, Earth's northern axis will shift away from Polaris and astronomers will assign a new North Star.[16]

Any discussion of Old Norse star constellations poses a vital question: did the Old Norse and Old Germanic peoples really see these constellations or are they modern reconstructions (or creations) based on Norse and Germanic myths? It likely that tribal groups, spread out over a large geographical area (and time), attributed different stories and meanings to the same (clusters of) stars, as was true for the Inuit people, spread over Greenland, Arctic Canada and Alaska.[17]

Much of the information available online is educated guess work, but I will now present what we know for sure. I have also created two Norse sky maps.

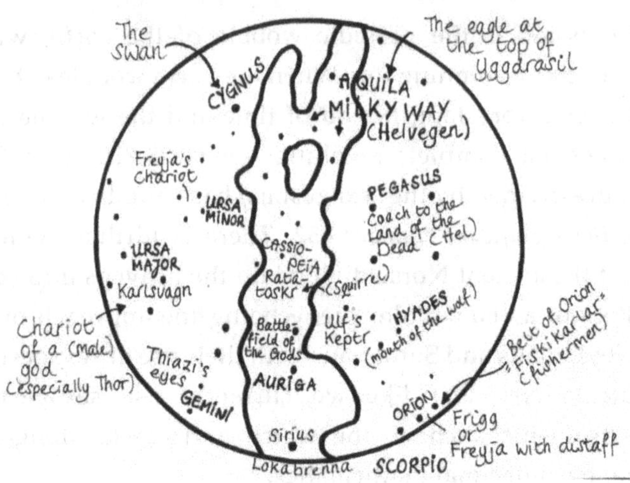

Norse Sky Map with the Milky Way as Helvegen

11 Norse Sky Map with the constellations as pictures

Day and Night

Most of us only see the stars at night (unless we live above the Arctic Circle and experience 24/7 darkness mid-winter.) *Dellingr* means dayspring or daybreak:

The father of Day// is Delling called
But Night was of Nörvi born;
Full moon and new moon//by the gods were fashioned
To tell the time for human beings
-Vafþrúðnismál, st. 25 *(Poetic Edda,* translation by author)

Day

Hail Day
Hail the sons of Day
Hail Night and her sister
With benevolent eyes look upon us
And give victory to us sitting here
(Author's own translation from Old Norse)

Night

The *Prose Edda* book *Gylfaginning* tells us that the goddess Nótt is a personification of Night. The figure High, on his throne, tells us that Nótt is the daughter of a jötunn called Norfi or Narfi. Nótt is described as *black and swarthy* and she has been married three times:

- Husband number one was Naglfari, they had one son called Auðr
- Next husband was Annar, resulting in a daughter called Jǫrð (Earth)

- Third husband is Dellingr (Dawn) and they have a son called Dagr (Day) who takes after his "father's people" in brightness and fairness

Odin placed both Nótt and her son Dagr in the sky. He gave them a chariot and horse each to circumnavigate Earth every 24 hours. Nótt rides ahead of Dagr, and foam from the bit of her horse *Hrímfaxi* (Frost Mane) sprinkles moisture on Earth. Dagr's horse is called *Skinfaxi* (Shining Mane). His mane lights up both sky and Earth.

The myth of Skinfaxi is now believed to have originated in the Nordic Bronze Age. It is believed that both horses interacted and exerted a pull on each other's movements: hence a rotation of day and night occurred.[18]

The Luminaries

Sól, the Sun

Sól and Máni are conceptualised as sister and brother. The Sun originated as a spark from Muspelheim.

The sun, the sister// of the moon, from the south
Her right hand cast// over heaven's rim;
No knowledge she had// where her home should be,
The moon knew not// what might was his,
The stars knew not// where their stations were.
Vǫluspá, st. 5

Both ride through the sky in horse-drawn chariots. Máni's horses remain unnamed but *Árvakr* (Early Awake) and *Alsviðr* (very swift), pull the chariot of Sól (the Sun). They move at great speed because both Sun and Moon are pursued by wolves, called Skoll (Mockery) and Hati (hate), who will overtake them at Ragnarok.

At this point in the creation story Mundilfari, the father of Sun and Moon becomes the Turner of Time.[19]

Máni, the Moon

Máni is the Moon.

Mundilfaeri is he// who began the moon,
And fathered the flaming sun//
The round of heaven each day they run//
To tell the time for men.
Vafþrúðnismál, st. 23

In *Alvíssmál,* the wise dwarf Alvis tells Thor that the moon is called "moon" by mankind, "fiery one" by the gods, "the whirling wheel" in Hel, "the hastener" by the jǫtnar, "the shiner" by the dwarves, and "the counter of years" by the elves.

Hjúki and Bil, attested in the *Prose Edda,* are the prototype for Jack and Jill in the famous nursery rhyme. They are the children of *Viðfinnr*. One day the children were walking home from a well called *Byrgir,* (Old Norse for *Hider of Something*), carrying a pole and a pail. Máni sweeps them up to the heavens and they can still be seen on the Moon. It has been suggested that Máni (in his chariot) represents the full moon, and the children embody the waxing and waning phases of the moon.[20]

We already met Hati but another source claims that a wolf called *Mánagarmr* ("Moon Hound") will swallow the moon and gorge on the dead. Some scholars believe that many different wolves mentioned in the Norse myths are Fenris.

Celestial Road or River

Irmin Street is the Milky Way, also known as Iring's Way, Walsingham Way, Bifrost of The Bridge of the Gods. There are some indications that world tree Yggdrasil might be the Milky Way.

Stars

The Lode Star (32 Camelopardis)

This star, known as Tir or the star of Tyr/Tiwaz, was the Pole Star in c. 800 CE. Our present Pole Star, Polaris, attained its special status in c. 1400 CE. This made it one of the *15 Behenian fixed stars of Medieval astronomy.*[21]

Polaris was known as the as *Leiðarstjarna* (lode-star) and the Anglo-Saxons called it the ship's star. Scandinavians viewed it as The God's Nail, associated with Thor.

Homes were once built around a central pillar dedicated to Thor. Nails were driven into this pole. The *axis mundi* (world axis) thus also became the central axis of a homestead. (Remember that in Scandinavia Polaris is directly overhead in the sky dome.)

In the Viking Era people also placed wooden pillars (*Öndvegissúlur*) on either side of the High Seat (meaning the place where the master and mistress of the household sat). Those high seat pillars had *reginnaglar* (Old Icelandic or "god-nails" or "power-nails") in them.

For the following listing of stars, I have (primarily) followed the list created by Nigel Pennick (in his book published in 1990) but I have added findings of my own.[22]

The Day Star (Arcturus, *alpha Bootis*) is also known as the *Bear Star.*

The South Star (Vega, alpha Lyrae) is used as a time marker and navigational aid.

The Torch *(Algol, Beta Persei)*

The Torch Bearer *(Procyon, alpha Canis Minor)*

Loki's Brand* or Lokabrenna *(Sirius, alpha Canis Major)* is situated at the base of the Milky Way. Sirius is the brightest star in the night sky and we now know that it is a binary system (it consists of two stars). For the Old Norse it was Loki's torch, referring to Midgard going up in flames, at Ragnarok.

Sirius is also known as the Dog Star, associated with the hottest days of summer in more southern cultures (e.g. Egypt). It heralded the (so called) dog days when crops would wilt, and people behaved badly or unpredictably.[23]

Constellations

The Big Dipper or the Plough is *Woden's (Odin's) Wagon* (Ursa Major or the Great Bear).

It is certain that the Old Norse and Germanic peoples viewed this as a wagon (REID). In different locations this wagon was associated with different gods (ASS). In some areas Odin was venerated as the chief god. Here we find *Óðins vagn* (Odin's wagon), also *vagna verr* (wagon's lord) and *valdr vagnbrautar* (ruler of the wagon-road).

Up to the 15th century Dutch people used the term *Woonswaghen* or *Woenswaghen,* as in: "*sevenstarre ofde Woenswaghen*" (the seven stars of Wodan's Wagon). Wednesday (*woensdag* in Dutch) is Odin's day and Ursa Major has seven stars.

Other areas were more focussed on Thor as the most powerful god. Here we find the '*Karlwagen*' or Karl's wagon. Karl was the familiar name given to Thor by Scandinavians. It is usually translated as *the old man,* also *Karla-Þórr,* Old Man Thórr. We also find '*Karlavagnen*': the (old) man's chariot.

> The God Thor was the highest of them// He sat naked as a child// Seven stars in his hand and Charles's Wain.
>
> *(Description of the statue of Thor at Uppsala)*[24]

Some authors claim that the seven stars could also point at the Pleiades, but the key evidence points at Ursa Major. The ancient goddess Nerthus was carried across fields (in ceremonial procession) in a wagon (REID) as well as rite of fertility and renewal.

***Our Lady's Wagon* (Ursa Minor or Little Bear)**

We find *Kvennavagn"* (the woman's chariot) for Ursa Minor. The gods associated most strongly with wagons were Thor and Freyja (the myths offer detailed descriptions). There are references to a throne as well. Ursa Minor looks a bit like a chair, but I often think the same thing about nearby Cassopeia.

***Frigg's Distaff* or *Freyja's Girdle, also Rejerock* or *Fröjas Rock* (the Belt of Orion)**

Friggerock (Frigg's distaff) refers to the three stars in 'the belt of Orion'. If we assume that people saw not only her distaff but also Frigg herself, Orion's 'sword' becomes a spindle pointing down). The information about *Friggerock* was obtained from people living in rural Sweden. Later the church fathers imposed the figure of Mother Mary on older representations of indigenous goddesses. This star cluster then becomes *Mariarock* instead, *the distaff of Maria,* the Heavenly Mother.

Freyja's magical necklace *Brisingamen* (made by the dwarfs) is sometimes referred to as a girdle and could have been worn as belt. I perceive it as a necklace made of stars.

The stars in Orion's belt were also known as *Fiskikarlar* (the fishermen) in Iceland and Norway, and in Germanic lands as *The Three Mowers.*[25]

Other Star Clusters

The following patterns are asterisms (star clusters), not formal star constellations.

***The Boar's Throng** (Pleiades or The Seven Stars)**

Taken from a Northern martial arts battle formation called *Svinfylking,* this is the warriors' wedge. This has the Lesser Wolf's Jaws facing a complex of stars called The Battle of the Gods.

The Battle of the Gods, (Asar Bardagi,* Auriga including the bright star Capella)

This demarcates the arena where the gods fight during Ragnarok.

***The Greater Wolf's Jaws* (Andromeda, part of the Milky Way, the semi-circle of stars through Pegasus to Cygnus, including Deneb Algedi*)**

The open jaws face the pole of the sky. This is the Fenris-wolf threatening the Cosmic Axis (Yggdrasil). There are two streams of saliva running down from The Greater Wolf's Jaws, called *Wil* and *Wan*.

***The Lesser Wolf's Jaws* (Hyades and Aldebaran*)**

Situated directly on the ecliptic, intercepting the Sun's path, these stars are perceived as violent and troublesome (other authors use the word evil), also associated with storms.[26]

Ulf's keptr (the Mouth of the Wolf)

This is an open star cluster known as the Hyades. It may have referred to Fenrir, but more likely referred to Garm, the wolf who guards the gates to the road to Hel (*Helvegen*), which is the Milky Way. (Some say both wolves are Fenris). This asterism appears in Taurus. The brightest stars form a distinct V shape (KEN).

Hellewagen (Wagon of the Dead)

This Germanic concept refers to the souls of the dead being transported across the Milky Way, to the ream of goddess Hel.

The most obvious candidate is Pegasus, located along the Milky Way.

Bifrost or Ásbrú (The trembling rainbow bridge or shimmering path)

The Milky Way may well be one manifestation of Bifrost (others are the rainbow, or the northern lights). The *Prose Edda* refers to it as Ásbrú (the bridge of the Aesir). It may have been a rainbow in the daytime and the Milky Way at night. Those phenomena opened portals to other realms.[27]

***Thiazi's Eyes* (the stars Castor and Pollux in Gemini)**

These two stars represent the eyes of a giant called *Thiazi*, thrown into the sky by Thor. They make a striking pair and sparkle with equal brightness on a winter night, thus reminding of eyes in the sky. This may be why they were associated with the winter goddess Skaði, as Thiazi was her father.[28]

***Aurvandil's Toe* (Corona Borealis, or its main star Alphecca*)**

Viewed as the toe of the giant Aurvandil (British spelling is Orwandil), once again thrown into the sky by Thor. The story is told in *Skáldskaparmál*.

Thor was summoned by Odin and challenged to fight Hrungnir, the strongest of all giants. He hurls Mjolnir at Hrungnir and meets a whetstone mid-air. It splinters and one piece gets stuck in Thor's head. Thor visits a wise woman, called Gróa, who sang her spells until the stone was loosened. Thor was so pleased to know she could get it out that he decided to reward Gróa. He told her that he had waded from the north over the river Élivága (Icy Stream) and had borne her husband Aurvandill in a basket on his back, out of Jotunnheim. He also explained that one of Aurvandill's toes stuck out of the basket and froze. So, Thor broke it off, cast it up into the heavens, and so created a star called Aurvandill's Toe. Gróa was so thrilled that she forgot her incantations. The whetstone remains stuck in Thor's head until today.[29]

Another theory suggests that Aurvandil's Toe is Venus. The old English name Éarendel is cognate with the Norse Aurvandil, and it refers to the morning star. Venus moves through phases of waxing and waning, just like the Moon. At times it appears in the sky as a bright crescent and does resemble a toenail.

The Danish historian Saxo Grammaticus (c. 1150 – 1220) wrote in Gesta Danorum about a figure called Horwendillus (Latinised from the Danish Ørvendil). Comparative studies of various related myths have led scholars to reconstruct a Common Germanic mythical figure named **Auza-wandilaz*, which seems to have personified the 'rising light' of the morning, possibly the Morning Star, which is, of course, Venus.[30]

The Behenian Fixed Stars

This is a list fifteen stars which were used for magical work in medieval astrology. Each was considered a source of power for one or more planets. We have already met some of them, but here is the complete list: *Algol, Alcyone, Aldebaran, Capella, Sirius, Procyon, Regulus, Alkaid, Algorab, Spica, Arcturus, Alphecca, Antares, Vega and Deneb Algedi.*

Ragnarok

The Old Norse constellations were markers of the seasons, connected to festivals and rituals. By the end of Autumn, the Torch Bearer announces the approach of Loki's Brand onto the Bridge of the Gods, where the Battle of the Gods is happening.

At midnight on the winter solstice, Loki's Brand stands at the southern end of Irmin Street (the Milky Way), with the Greater Wolf's Jaws and Orwandil's Toe situated directly opposite each other as vernal and autumn constellations. Twelvetide is a time of cosmic danger!

Four Stags or Harts

An eagle sits in the branches of the ash, and it has knowledge of many things, and between its eyes sits a hawk called *Vedrfolnir*. A squirrel called *Ratatoskr* runs up and down through the ash and carries malicious messages between the eagle and *Nidhoggr*. Four stags run in the branches of the ash and feed on the foliage.[31]

The poems *Grímnismál* and *Gylfaginning* in the *Poetic Edda* describes four stags or harts (male red dear) nibbling on the branches of the world tree. The morning dew gathers in their horns and forms the rivers of our world.

It has been suggested that Cassiopeia was the squirrel *Ratatoskr* (Drill Tooth), who runs up and down the tree passing messages between the Eagle (linked to the modern swan constellation Cygnus) at the top of the tree and the serpent gnawing on the bottom of the tree, Níðhǫggr (which has been connected to Scorpio).

Chapter 10

The Runes and Old Norse Anatomy of Soul

Medicine rests upon four pillars – philosophy, astronomy, alchemy, and ethics.

-Paracelsus

Modern Western culture perceives the human soul as one unique totality, separate from the souls of other people. The Old Norse people had a different "anatomy of soul". For them, souls had different parts, performing different roles. This chapter explains this and asks: do parts of the human soul have a natural affiliation with certain runes?

Sál

Astrologers view the natal chart as a blueprint of the human soul. As a rune magician I often work with a Norse soul map and place runes on it, to gain insight into deeper issues and patterns in human lives. A soul map is divided into Norse "parts of the soul" (like segments of an orange). Placing runes there indicates in which areas of a soul significant action, interaction or transformation is happening.

The Old Norse word for "soul" (as in one unified entity), *sál*, was invented only after Christianisation so it did not exist previously.[1]

The Old Norse people believed that the 'body was in the soul' rather than the 'soul being in the body'. Their perception of soul was more porous and expansive than our modern one. Matters relating to our physical body, as well as family, kin and ancestors *also* show up in the larger constellation of soul. In other words: *some aspects of our soul are transpersonal and collective.*

I teach my advanced students of *Seiðr* how to place runes on the soul map and do readings for clients. That work can only be done safely by well-trained people, so I am not sharing the method here, but this chapter generally explores runes in the context of the Old Norse anatomy of soul. I am indebted to Raven Kaldera for the concept of a soul map.[2]

The First Human Beings

To examine the Norse aspects of soul we start with a creation story:

> One day Odin and his brothers (Villi and Vé) were walking on a beach. The gods found two trees (driftwood) from which they created the first human beings, Askr and Embla, who were not (yet) capable of anything. The gods decide to give them certain qualities, but scholars still debate exactly what they were.

The modern consensus is that:

> Odin gave them breath and spirit [*Ǫnd, óðr*].
> Vili gave movement, intelligence, behaviour [*Læti*].
> Vé gave them shape, speech and hearing (possibly all their senses) [*La*].
> Odin's name means breath and by extension spirit. Vili's name relates to will and will-power (the Old Norse word Villi) and Vé means sacred space. The sequence suggests that the gods gifted humans a soul/spirit and free will, in a sacred place or space. The rune correspondences are obvious:
> Odin's rune is ASS (breath, soul, spirit). Movement is REID and we find the human will, driving all human creations and civilisations at MADR. Sacred space is

ODAL: personal and ancestral home, but also a space with boundaries (dividing "in" from "out"). A sanctuary or sacred space.

Aspects of Soul

Exactly how many aspects of soul exist remains debatable. It depends on how you "cut the pizza" and how you count. I prefer to use the largest number of possibilities on the soul map I created, because this works well for intense and detailed readings. Please conceptualize the entire constellation of "soul" as a large pizza that has been chopped up into digestible slices.

LIK refers to the physical body (though it is etymologically related to the modern word for corpse in Germanic languages. In contemporary Swedish the noun "lik" means corpse).

Holistic health disciplines teach that *matters related to our body originate in our soul* (and mind, psyche). Any disease ("dis-ease", not at ease) indicates an imbalance. This could be personal (shaped by personal history, such as childhood adversity), relate to our ancestral field or to environmental and geopolitical issues.

Then there are local and global imbalances. Do we live in a time of peace or armed conflict; a time of prosperity or famine? Has our land been invaded or colonized?

The Norse creation story provides the segments for looking at all these aspects under Ǫnd/Óðr, Litr, Laeti and La.

The adjective Óðr means Divine Madness: frantic, furious or vehement. Odin was "the frenzied one". As a noun it refers to the mind, feelings, song and poetry. That is a touching description of the human soul.[3]

HAMR means shape and refers to semi-physical body images, sometimes called *the energy body*. Karmic or ancestral imprints and diseases are carried in this aspect of soul, visible to healers and shamans.

HUGR refers to our conscious mind and cognitive function.

MINNI is personal memory and our faculty for self-reflection but it also includes the vast collective well of ancestral memories (which I connect to Urðarbrunnr, Urdr's Well).

HAMINGJA is the concept of luck (or good fortune) as a personal possession we can nurture. Unlike modern Western culture it is not a case of being lucky or unlucky (and having no power or control over that). It is something we can actively work with, nurture, stabilise or even top up with good deeds. It is a dynamic and empowering "substance" which also provides protection and the ability to shape shift.

The following aspects are (even more) nebulous and multi-dimensional (or multi-purpose) but I still consult them on the soul map:

SKUGGI (and/or VÅLNE) Skuggi means shadow. It is our shade, our energetic (astral) shape or manifestation which survives physical death. You could also say that this is our HAMR continuing after death, in a more spectral form, when it no longer receives energy from our physical body. I also use this (in a modern sense) as the place indicating where shadow work needs to be done.

MOD refers to our feelings. Not so much fleeting and ever-changing emotions as our underlying core feelings; the mood we rest in when nothing lifts or torpedoes our spirits. I use it to read emotional health and to see how unresolved ancestral emotions (residues) and themes remain potent or active in our lives.

MEGIN means personal power. This position will provide a reading on both how (emotionally, spiritually and motivationally) empowered we are and how well we manage our physical health, to support our mission in the world. (This aspect links back to LITR).

FYLGJA and KINFYLGJA, literally mean the *Following Spirit* and *Clan Spirit*. The *Fylgja* is the tutelary and protective spirit watching over individuals (similar to a Fetch in Irish folklore). It can also refer to the afterbirth of a child (the "follower", born next).

The *Kinfylgja* performs the same role for an entire family, clan or kinship group. Psychic people can perceive them near us. We can ask them for guidance and actively work on our relationship with them.

Old Norse sagas tell us that the fylgja could assume animal shape or human form. The animal fylgja is said to appear in front of its owner, often in dreams, as an omen or portent of events to come (often death, note the link to fate).

Egil's Saga offers description of both Egil and his father Skallagrim transforming into wolves or bears. This touches on the phenomenon of *berserking*: wilfully shapeshifting into an animal to take on the characteristics and powers of that animal.

All scholars (and practitioners) will have their own lens of perception. Norwegian philologist Else Mundal claimed that the female *Fylgja* could also be considered a *Dís*, defined by her as a ghost or goddess attached to fate. (I strongly prefer the term *compassionate ancestor* to "ghost" in this context!) On a related note, I also look at the positions of the Valkyria and Godi or Gydja on my map, where the Valkyria represents our inner warrior and our relationship to death.

GOÐI and GYÐJA are the words for priest and priestess, human roles in spiritual matters. I use those positions to look at my clients' relationship with deities, spirits and other worlds. Are they fully empowered spiritually speaking? Can they act as their own priest(ess)?

URÐR (the word becomes Wyrd in Old English) is the place of the Norns carving our fate. The origin of all patterns. The things we cannot change in this lifetime but need to live with or around.

ØRLǪG literally means primal law and it looks at what has already been carved: what has come to pass, been set in motion. How does our personal fate intersect and interact with other people (and all beings)?

ODAL is the domain of ancestral land/soul/heritage/connection and feeling at home. I use this position to look at matters of belonging, the way ancestral imprints play out in our choices and decisions and the places our soul calls home.

The Runes of Soul

Of course, all runes are runes of the human soul, but some refer to very specific domains of soul:

LIK – MADR
Physical existence, the human condition.
ǪND, ÓÐR – ASS
Spirit (but also our mother tongue or first language).
LITR, LAETI and LA – REID
Movement, motion and velocity.

Specific rune axes of soul
(Part II of this book lists all soul axes in dictionary format.)

HAMR – THURS (hurt, harm, intrusions, boundary violations and diseases).

KEN (ordeals and initiations), even LAGU: our energy field acts as a mirror of the sum of all we are, feel and experience.

HUGR – ASS (in a spirit-led life), TYR (in a courageous person), IS (as the capacity for deep reflection and gaining clarity).

MINNI – LAGU and LAGU – MADR (access to personal and ancestral memories).

HAMINGJA – WYNJA and WYNJA – MADR (do I and did my ancestors increase the family fortune by good deeds and living honorably?)

SKUGGI (and/or VÅLNE): This refers to the shape or energetic form of a person after death. However, practitioners of folk magic also summon the vålne or vålnad (SW) of a person, meaning their energetic "gestalt", when a crime has been committed, to identify the criminal.[4]

MOD: MADR – LAGU
Individual and collective feelings. Here I read emotional health and the presence of ancestral residues (general unresolved trauma).

MEGIN: THURS – MADR, LAGU
Megin means personal power. I read how empowered clients are and how well they manage their physical health. This aspect links back to LITR.

FYLGJA and KINFYLGJA: ASS, ASS – MADR and ASS – ODAL

Here we read how spirit helpers watch over us and our home and clan (or chosen kinship group). We can be an active relationship with them and ask for daily guidance.

VALKYRIA: TYR – EH

Our inner spiritual warrior, choosing the hill we die on, where our passion transcends personal death.

GOÐI and GYÐJA: ASS – ALGIZ.

Is a person spiritually independent? Authenticity and standing in your spiritual power.

URÐR: NAUD – MADR

The place where fate shows up. The origin of unchangeable patterns. The things we cannot change in this lifetime, but need to make our peace with and live with, or live around.

ØRLǪG: NAUD – MADR – ODAL

Literally primal law: *what has already been carved.* How does our personal fate intersect and interact with other people (and other actors such an animal, land, property, local laws, geo-political powers etc.)

ODAL: MADR – ODAL

This is the domain of ancestral land/soul/heritage/connection and knowing where we belong. It casts lights on matters of belonging and the places our soul calls home.

Soul Map Work by Rune

- UR: All things primal and primordial.
- THURS: Ymir & our Giant Ancestors & Lineage.
- ASS: Our relationship to spirit, religion or belief system.
- REID: Physical movement and spiritual journey, stories we tell ourselves and scripts we follow, our favourite music.
- KEN: Our "inner blacksmith" forging our character through hammering (ordeals, initiations, crises).
- GIFU: Sacred reciprocity, do we give as much as we receive? Psychologists say that a key factor in healthy relationships is balanced, healthy and rewarding relationships with others.
- WYNJA: Our greatest joy, following our bliss or the lodestar of our soul.
- HAGAL: Tests of character, our ability to handle adversity and make comebacks (rebirth ourselves).
- NAUD: Our relationship with both The Norns and our personal norn.
- IS: Fearless Introspection, time on ice, solitude.
- JARA: Harvest and scythe, bringing things to fruition, cycles of sowing and reaping. Also accepting times of decline or "having less".
- PERTHRA: Cave time.
- EOH: Axis mundi, moral compass.
- ALGIZ: Fylgja and animal self, animal powers, "finding our antlers", shapeshifting.
- SOL: Heat and warmth, our solar self, shining our light, contributing our unique gifts to the collective.
- TYR: Courage, inner spiritual warrior.
- BJARKA: Our inner healer and herbalist, maternal instincts, parenting, mentoring, nurturing young lives.

- EH: Our relationship with death and otherworld journeys; partnerships with others, marriage and endings of relationships. (The axis of divorce is GIFU – EH).
- MADR: the human condition, ontological questions, our relationship with other human beings and our ancestors.
- LAGU: memories, emotions, ability to be in flow and go with the flow.
- ING: seeds, (MADR – ING = human potential).
- ODAL: home, belonging, roots, enclosed space, home country. (ODAL – ASS is our mother tongue).
- DAGAZ: evolution of soul and enlightenment, seeing the higher perspective, holding two opposing views or conflicting truths in mind at the same time.
- FE: money matters but also psychological and intellectual wealth: self-esteem, original ideas (FE – ASS), the skills we use to support ourselves (KEN – FE).

Creating Your Own Formats for Rune Readings

Popular formats exist, e.g. pull three runes and do a "Norn Spread", where a rune is pulled for each Norn (representing past, present and future) but obviously I do not translate the names of the Norns that way. Therefore the templates I teach my students look very different.

Having said that, the options are truly unlimited! Meditate on the deities you work with, e.g. pull runes for Freyja and Skadi. Put runes on your own cognitive map of Yggdrasil (cradling all worlds). Use a rune to give voice to let any character from Norse cosmology "speak".

Freya Aswynn uses runes to map the non-Norse concepts of the seven cardinal sins (and links them to the seven traditional planets of astrology). You could even place runes on your natal chart (or any other chart) for further elucidation.[5]

War and Peace

Students often ask whether runes are for personal use only or whether they can be also be used for global situations. There is nothing to stop you from doing a rune reading on a global situation or conflict (though I know I would end up pulling many extra runes for clarification).

While working on this book Russia invaded Ukraine. I am typing this chapter in Sweden, a neighbouring country across the Baltic Sea. The Israel-Palestine conflict also escalated into ever greater violence.

Globally speaking the list of places where humanitarian disasters and grave human rights violations occur is never-ending. I wrote a long essay about this in 2024.[6]

I teach all my students that consent (from the receiving party) is required before they can put prayer requests on my altar. However, from my Roman Catholic childhood I know that many well-meaning Christians pray for every person and cause that comes to their attention. Ultimately this is matter of belief system: if I believe that prayer is a form of spiritual work which might have some effect on outcomes (as I do), then my personal code of ethics demands consent.[7]

When I chant the runes every morning, I always ask that any person, who wishes to be included, is woven in. (I don't need to know their names or location, the spirits take care of that). I include prayer requests shared on social media and in groups I am a member of.

The runes can be used by any individuals, anywhere, who feel drawn to them. They can be used in protection magic and for calling in powerful deities.

When Russia invaded Ukraine, I admit that I felt a strong urge to ask Norse deities to rush to the defense of Ukraine and place protection runes on maps (emotional response). I immediately had second thoughts about this. I am not Ukrainian. The Norse gods are not Ukrainian. No one with a personal connection to Ukraine has asked me to do this, so my personal Code of Ethics tells me to stay clear. (But the internet informed me that there is an initiative where magicians work magic for Ukrainian children on video calls!)

Chapter Exercise

In modern Western society we often use the word soul. How do you define your concept of soul? Attempt to write down a definition.

When this is done, write down your own definition of spirit. How is it different from soul?

Chapter 11

The Runes as Medicine

"Rune Vaccine"

The Runes as Healers

When the Covid-19 Pandemic started I created the sigil above to call in the power of all the runes. Chanting all runes is one way of returning something to its state of primordial or divine perfection.

Every rune has healing properties. As healing is generally about restoring balance where there is imbalance, disharmony (or even disease) it might be better to say that they have balancing properties. Below is a list of what they can amplify or activate:

- UR – *Back to the drawing board, rewilding.*
- THURS – Protection: placing a boundary/shield/force or even deity (Thor) between us (or vulnerable people/

places) and danger. Healing wounds and trauma. Standing up for what we believe in. Sacred activism (without hurting or harming others). Planting a thorny hedge around our homestead to keep out intruders.

- ASS – Artistic inspiration, creativity, opening our connection to Spirit, committing to a spirit-led life. In a secular society this piece atrophies in many people.
- REID – Breaking up what is rigid or stagnant, getting things moving (again), accepting the cyclical nature of life and relationships (including our relationship to ourselves).
- KEN – Surrendering to initiation and ordeals, allowing ourselves to be "forged" by otherworld blacksmiths (baptisms of fire), accessing the qualities of steel and iron within ourselves, increasing will power and endurance.
- GIFU – Reflecting deeply on the quality of sacred reciprocity, doing better in relationships, becoming a good (or better) marriage partner or friend, healing wounds in relationships, recovering from betrayals or infidelity.
- WYNJA – Inviting more joy; a good rune for people suffering from depression to physically carry on their person. Place on our personal altar for domestic peace, harmony, abundance, joy, a contented life.
- HAGAL – Think very carefully about activating Hagal Medicine by choice, in either our own lives or the lives of others. Always consider Ørlǫg (the karmic consequences, the fact the Norns carve fate, are your treading on their territory?) HAGAL is best used when people are already in a process of rebirth, but this gets stalled, and they get stuck in a very uncomfortable place. Activating Hagal or the Pregnant Hag can get them unstuck, but this requires a serious turbulence warning

(things will get worse before they get significantly better).

- NAUD – Rune of the Norns, so act with caution. A good rune to invoke when a debate about ethics and long-term consequences is badly needed (examples are contemporary debates about AI, cloning, genetically modified crops, genetic modification of human DNA etc.)
- IS – Creating time on ice, cooling, clarity and deep contemplation. Use with warring couples, hotheaded people who need to learn to think before they act etc. Use as a knife to cut through confusion or obfuscation. It can also be used to reflect bitter truths: e.g. is there a narcissist involved in this situation? Perhaps not all participants are playing the same rule book?
- JARA – Rune of the Harvest. Some shamanic healing clients have literally said to me: "I keep planning seeds, but the harvest never comes." This rune can be used to bring projects or resolutions to fruition, to see through an entire cycle without bad planning, distraction of self-sabotage.
- PERTHRA – Use when Cave Time is needed. For someone who needs to retreat and rebirth themselves in the cosmic womb.
- EOH – Use when a strong axis is needed: setting priorities (what do I want my life tp evolve around, what is the central focus?) Be careful if you decide to work with the meaning of yew: it is a highly poisonous tree, found in graveyards. It can be used to call in transcendence, life triumphing over death, but you need to know what you are doing. Measured doses of yew-derived medicine are used in chemotherapy.
- ALGIZ – A good rune to use to enhance our connection to spirit, especially animal spirits and powers. Allow this

rune to pull you away from your computer, out of your darkened and air-conditioned (or heated) room and into the forest and other wild spaces. Use it to invoke antlered or horned gods.

- SOL – A great rune for children (or adults) who spend too much time behind computers. Pull them out into the sunshine so their body produces vitamin D. Start every day with sunshine on your skin. This will regulate the melatonin cycle and help you sleep at night.
- TYR – Use for finding courage, putting the needs of others above our own (and even for contacting wolf powers!) Shadow work: reflecting on oaths and bonds and sacred promises (and how we may have broken those).
- BJARKA – Great rune for anyone who runs women's groups or circles. Contacting the mysteries of the sacred feminine. Awakening healing abilities, our inner herbalist, apothecary.
- EH – Be careful around the core meaning death, but a good companion for people navigating symbolic death or reaching end-of-life care. Also, the rune of twins and partnerships. Can be used to attract or partnerships or forge stronger bonds ("Until death do us part").
- MADR – Especially useful in ancestral healing work. It can also be used to put focus on humanitarian causes. Good medicine for people who need to heal grandiosity (or self-obsession) and learn humility, the importance of other people and human connections, of being in service to others.
- LAGU – Make potions and bring greater flow. Unlock emotions. Enhance the ability to dream (and remember dreams). Good for rigid people who need to learn about going with the flow and achieving flow states.

- ING – Use in the garden while planting seeds. I sing ING songs to my seedlings and plants. I chant ING songs in the forest after logging has occurred. Use to unlock human potential. Use to awaken our sexuality and learn how to live in a sexual universe.
- ODAL – Use to make an existing home stronger or manifest a home for a homeless or dispossessed person/ group of people. Can help us delineate what is in and what is out: where to draw boundaries around our private lives (also on the internet and social media, our virtual home or classroom etc.)
- DAGAZ – For spiritual people chasing enlightenment. Casting light in dark corners or on murky situations (investigative journalism, police work, psychotherapy). Can help us focus on the ultimate oneness of everything, seeing the larger picture, the higher perspective or greater good.
- FE – Unless you are a cattle farmer, use this rune to manifest money, help yourself value your own time and services, asking for a pay rise. Balancing or healing our financial situation. Paying off debts. (The Old Norse word *manngjǫld* becomes wergild in English, literally "man payment").

Using Runes in Healing – Practical Suggestions:

The options are unlimited (get creative!) but here are some suggestions to get you started:

- Make personalized runes for clients to carry on their person (e.g. necklace or amulet in pocket).
- Paint or draw runes on your own or another person's body (consent is obviously required.) Or place runes on a person's body in a session.

- Invite a client to intuitively pull runes and place them on their own body (a very interesting way of doing a rune reading, as it gives you both a rune and body part. Both have significance.)
- Working with non-humans: place runes on the land, a tree stump or a (world) map etc.
- Make a wand or staff with runes carved on it.
- Draw runes in the Earth (or in the air if it is not appropriate to touch anything)
- Use your voice to chant runes.
- Chanting the entire circle of runes is said to pull all of creation back to its original perfection.
- Work with the ancient principle that food is medicine. Draw runes over food or drink as a blessing, to express gratitude and activate its healing potential.
- Draw a rune and put a bottle of water on it for a night to make an (almost homeopathic) rune potion, water with an energetic rune signature.

Runic Axes

The next level is working with Runic Axes, see part II of this book.

Bind Runes

By combining two runes (or more), we can also make bind runes and create powerful personalized symbols. Some people make logos, print them on T shirts or embroider them on ceremonial cloaks or altar cloths. Others wear them as tattoos. The possibilities are endless.

God Staves

Try making "god staves", beautiful graphics honoring a particular deity. Runes can in incorporated in that (e.g. IS for Skadi or THURS for Thor etc.)

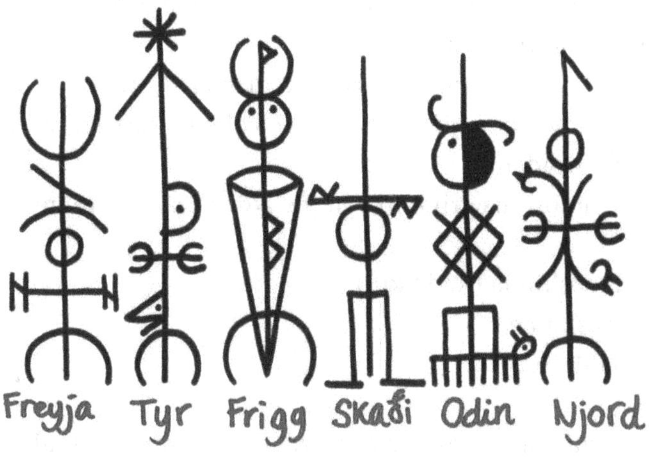

God Staves

Note from my Rune Journal: *does a god live in every place where two lines intersect?*

Sigils

We already encountered basic sigils earlier. Sigils can become incredibly complex and intricate, holding many layers of meaning. They are condensed images used in magical workings. They may contain the energy signature of a deity or helping spirit. In medieval times they often represented angels and demons. The word sigil is derived from a Latin word meaning seal (as in sealing a document, not the animal).

Grimoires

We find many sigils in grimoires, magical books where practitioners kept a record of their work. These books were studied by later generations of practitioners as manuals for their own training and magical operations.

After Christianization, especially during period of the Inquisition and the dark age of the witch trials, heathen traditions were suppressed, and many magical books were burned or hidden in attics.

There used to be a thriving grimoire tradition in the Scandinavian countries. They are called *svarteböcker* (black books) in Sweden.

Some notorious grimoires in the Northern Tradition are:

- Rauðskinna (Red Skin)
- Gráskinna
- Galdrabók

Rauðskinna is about gaining control over Satan. It was allegedly to have been buried with its author, the Bishop Gottskálk grimmi Nikulásson of Hólar in Iceland. Gráskinna (Grey Skin) contains spells mastered by the magician Galdra-Loftur, Loftur Þorsteinsson, in 18th century Iceland. Galdrabók is the oldest and most complete book we have. This collection of magical spells was written in Iceland in the late 1500s (the Reformation Age). It contains two different types of spells: prayer formulas invoking supernatural powers and spells to manifest the magician's will.[1]

Magic in the Eddas and Sagas

Egill Skallagrímsson was a Viking Era poet, sorcerer, berserker and farmer. Egil was the grandson of Kveld-Úlfr (whose name means "Evening Wolf"). Another of his ancestors, Hallbjörn, was Norwegian-Sami.[2]

Egill was also a master rune magician. Egil's Saga describes the period from 850 – 1000 CE and it provides both inspiration and warnings. He was asked to visit a sick woman. A local landowner had been refused her hand in marriage, and he had resorted to working love magic. He was not competent, so he ended up carving runes for invoking sickness instead. Egil burned these runes and carves runes for health instead. The woman made a full recovery.

Egil also used runes while a raising a *Níðstang* (cursing pole) against King Eirik Bloodaxe and Queen Gunnhildr. This is a long wooden pole with a fresh horse head pinned at the top, sometimes with the skin of the horse laid over the pole. He carved runes on it and the pole was pointed in the direction of target of this curse.

Sacred Trees and Types of Wood

Rune work did not stand alone. The type of wood that runes were carved on added its own significance. Wood would have been harvested intentionally and ceremonially (my own primary rune set was made from a Juniper struck by lightning, meaning that it carries a strong Juniper and Thor signature.)

In pre-Christian Scandinavia trees were believed to have magical powers. Unusually shaped trees were particularly good for working magic, especially trees that offered a natural hole or portal. Sick people were pulled through that hole while magical formulas spoken or chanted.

There were also *värkträd,* trees used to extract pain from a human body part. (But the careless person who cut down the tree ended up carrying all the pain!)[3]

- Alder wood is both water-loving and resistant (good for foundations of buildings in watery locations). It is a source of bright dyes (orange-red sap is associated with blood and war), otherworld journey and smoking meat.[4]
- Aspen quakes and it whispers. Its bark contains analgesic and anti-inflammatory properties. It grows in places decimated by forest fires or logging. A rod of aspen called a "fe" was used to measure graves.
- In Scandinavia *Askefrun* (Ash Woman) is said to reside in the ash tree (or under its roots). She was feared but as a protective spirit she was offered food and drink. She could send people illness if she was displeased.[5]

- The Swedish name for a beech tree is *bok* (literally book). It represents learning and preserving knowledge, as a threshold tree.
- Birch trees ward off bad energies, banish fears, build courage, beauty and tolerance. Also new beginnings (pioneer tree), the wood was used to make cradles for babies.
- The Elder is called *Hyllemor* in Sweden and Denmark. It is the tree of witches (Rune HAGAL) and a veritable medicine chest. Her indwelling spirit is a Crone, the Pregnant Hag. She was planted in cemeteries (in Europe) to keep bad spirits away
- Hazel wands are used for magic and healing and forked sticks are used for finding water. Wood heightens the senses, poetry and creativity, deep dreaming.
- Juniper is used for protection, seeking visions, clarity, wisdom and prosperity. The berries can be used in amulets.
- Pine is an evergreen with many medicinal properties: antiseptic, expectorant, and tonic. Needles and cones are harvested. New life, long life, strength.
- Rowan (mountain ash): the wood was used to make spindles and spinning wheels, also divining rods. Rowan berries are used in magic, for protection amulets against bad spirits and illness.
- "Flying Rowan" (*flygrönn*): a rowan sapling growing in another tree without ever touching the ground. Said to protect against thunder and lightning and the magical workings of others (*trolldom*). I also use it for flying magic, helping projects take off and soar.
- Willow contains salicylic acid, used to make aspirin. Wands are used to invoke vivid dreams and drawing down the moon (it is a lunar tree due to its close connection with water). Witch's brooms are bound with a willow branch. Tree of prophecy and seership.

- Yew is about transcendence, regeneration, resurrection and eternal life. Used in spells to summon the dead (necromancy) and divination. Very poisonous. Contains Taxol (which inhibits cancer cells). It is called the Forbidden Tree because it was used to bring on abortion.

Do Runes Represent Deities?

Did every rune originally represent a deity or Divine being? Some runes clearly represent deities. Perhaps the most obvious ones are Ass (Ansuz), sometimes called The God Rune and Tyr (the Rune of the Spiritual Warrior). I put forward the following list:

1. UR (Uruz) – Adhumbla and Norn Urðr
2. THURS (Thurisaz) – Thor and the Thursar
3. ASS (Ansuz) – The God Rune, the Rune of Odin and Aesir gods
4. REID (Raidho) – Time as a Divinity, Reidatyr
5. KEN – The Sons of Ivaldi, and Brokkr
6. GIFU – Gefjon/Gefjun
7. WYNJA – Frigg
8. HAGAL – Hel, Freyja (and all witches), the Pregnant Hag
9. NAUD (Nauthiz) – the Norns (as the Mothers/Powers of Necessity) and Loki
10. IS (Isa) – Rune of Skadi and the Frost Giants
11. JARA (Jera) – Fjǫrgyn/Jörð and Sif
12. PERTHRA – Bergsrå (the Mountain Mother or Mountain King)
13. EOH – Ullr, Yggdrasil and the Iviðja

Maria Kvilhaug gives us the iviðja or Witch-Within-Wood and identifies her as the ancient Vǫlva, who speaks in the Vǫluspá:

... the Witch Within Wood
Brings forth the ages...
-Hrafnagalðr Oðinns

14. ALGIZ = The Alcis *(Also, the Celestial Elk Mother of indigenous Siberian peoples)*
15. SOL = Sunna and Sol, also Dellingr
16. TYR = spiritual warrior god Tyr
17. BJARKA – Birch Tree, Mother
18. EH – Sleipnir and Svaðilfari
19. LAGU – An Early Divinity conceptualized as Mother Water, or the Lady of the Lake. Viking Era: Rán, Aegir and Njord
20. Ing – Freyr
21. Odal – The Landvaettir, Gårdstomte and Tomptaghud
22. DAGAZ – Dagr
23. FE – Eggþér

Eggþér (Edge Servant) is a Giant and Herdsman who sits on a mound, joyfully playing his harp, while the red rooster Fjalar begins to crow, heralding the onset of Ragnarok.

I will court controversy by saying that this is another indication that FE is the final rune and not the first rune.

He sat on the mound and plucked his harp
the herdsman of the giantess, cheerful Eggther
a rooster crowed in Gallows-wood
that bright-red cockerel who is called Fialar
— Vǫluspá St. 42 (Larrington translation)

I am intrigued by the meaning of his name: Edge Servant. Some believe this refers to his job of inciting the jötnar and wolves to battle during Ragnarök. It clearly indicates someone in service to a highly liminal place. What is a more liminal place than the space between two worlds in time, or between two universes?

The multiverse is the hypothetical set of all universes. Together, these universes are presumed to comprise everything that exists: the entirety of the space-time continuum including the physical laws and mathematical constants that describe it. The different universes within the multiverse are called "parallel universes", "other universes", "alternate universes", or "many worlds". One common assumption is that the multiverse is a "patchwork quilt of separate universes all bound by the same laws of physics.

Chapter 12

From the Stone Age to Modern Mysticism

The conundrum of writing any book is choosing what is going to be *left out*. We need to tie up some loose ends and answer some frequently asked questions before describing rune axes in more detail.

Did Old Norse People Practice Shamanism?

Shamanism is a word derived from the Manchu-Tungus word šaman. It means "one who knows" or "one who sees". It was adopted by Russian people who interacted with the indigenous peoples of Siberia. The English word shamanism was coined in 1780, by adding *-ism* to this word.

We live in a time where cultural appropriation has been exposed widely (also situations where cross-fertilization might be a more correct word). The word *shamanism* has fallen out of grace.

The Old Norse peoples had their own words for their magical practices and "spiritual technology": *seiðr* and *trolldomr.* People commonly refer to this diverse body of knowledge as "Norse Shamanism". This is anachronistic and it upsets people who take issue with the word shamanism. I educate all my students about these matters – but I cannot put words in their mouths.

I still speak of two decades of healing work (in inner city London) as my "shamanic practice", because I offered *shamanic healing sessions* and that was the energy signature. I have also published two books with shamanism in the title. It's not possible to edit those things after the fact. If I started this work now, I would (probably) speak of spirit-led healing sessions and spirit work. In the perfect scenario, I would work exclusively within a Nordic/Old Norse framework and use terms from Old Norse and modern Scandinavian languages.

The Sacred Feminine in Norse Cosmology

People often complain that the Norse pantheon is very male-dominated but I hope this book demonstrates how the sacred feminine is equally present (if we scratch below the surface).

For readers who work with the sacred feminine, one day I decided to map Her presence in the rune row:

- UR is the primordial Cow Mother suckling Ymir.
- ASS references the vǫlur (plural of vǫlva) Odin wakes in their graves and speaks to about prophetic matters.
- GIFU is the Goddess of the Land marrying the King of the Land.
- WYNJA is Frigg, presiding over home and hearth.
- HAGAL is the dark goddess, bringer of sacred destruction in service to creation.
- NAUD represents the fate-carving Norns, more powerful even than the gods.
- IS is Skaði, the Winter Goddess, who travels on skis accompanied by wolves.
- JARA is Sif, the goddess with golden tresses and wife of Thor (in his manifestation of a god of rain and storms, a ruler of the harvest).
- PERTHRA is the Mountain Mother who receives *bergtagen* people with open arms.
- EOH is the axis mundi around which everything rotates. In homes all over the world this role often falls to the mother ("mater familias").
- ALGIZ is the Reindeer Mother who carries the Sun in her antlers at the Winter Solstice.
- SOL is Sunna, who will produce a daughter at Ragnarok so the next world (or universe) will have a sun too.

- TYR: Archaeologists have discovered that there were many female warriors in the Viking Age. Those women were highly regarded and buried with impressive grave goods. All women have an inner spiritual warrior.
- BJARKA is the Birch Mother presiding over all women's mysteries. Many healers and herbalists are women.
- EH: Ordinary people who die a straw death (in their own bed, not a warrior's death) go to Helheim. The goddess Hel receives them and treats them well. Her hall is *not* a realm of punishment and damnation.
- MADR: Women make up 49.6% of the world population but 106 boys are born for every 100 girls. This means that at a certain (fertile) age the number balances out but then becomes less balanced again in old age. Women tend to outlive men as there is a 5-year gap in average life expectancy.
- LAGU is Rán, the goddess who claims those who die at sea.
- ING represents fertility and pregnant women.
- ODAL: In the Viking Age the homestead was the realm of a powerful woman who kept all keys, to all cupboards, buildings and storage units, on her belt.
- DAGAZ refers to the sacred balance of sacred feminine and sacred masculine and an enlightened perspective.
- FE: The abundance of cattle pivots on cows.

Which Runes Are "Shamans"?

Some students have asked me "which runes are the (so called) shamans?" So I made the list below. Using transformative power as the keystone, all runes earn their place in this category. Human beings can work with any rune and derive immense "shamanic" power from this partnership.

- UR = to me is Norn Urdr and the primordial Volva who speaks in the Voluspa.
- THURS = Thor is an herbalist and healer.
- ASS = Odin is a "shaman", wisdom seeker and psychopomp.
- REID = the Rune of Time and the Great Mover, of issues healing themselves through repetition and of healing stories.
- KEN = Blacksmith as Shaman.
- GIFU = the sacred marriage of the goddess and the returning warrior priest ("shamanic" figures).
- WYNJA = Frigg sees everything but does not speak of what she sees (a silent prophetess).
- HAGAL = The Witch, the Pregnant Hag, the Medicine Woman, the Shape Shifter who knows the secrets of rebirthing herself.
- NAUD = human "shamans" only have prophetic powers courtesy of the Norns.
- IS = is an icicle used as a scalpel, and refers to all tools used by shamans to see deeply into the heart of any matter or sharp tools used to perform extraction work.
- JARA = the Harvest Mother, a manifestations of the Earth Mother who provides food for her offspring.
- PERTHRA= The Mountain Mother and the realm of the dwarfs, artisans crafting magical tools for the gods.
- EOH = ingredients harvested from the yew tree are used in chemotherapy (saving or prolonging lives through shrinking tumors and killing off cancer cells). A modern (medically advanced) way of healing. In the right dose toxic substances can be medicine.
- ALGIZ = The Lord of Animals or Wild Adversary as Shaman
- SOL = The life-giving principle. In Andean shamanism people call themselves "the children of the Sun".

Sunna is not a shaman but she can be said to give human beings their luminosity, their ability to shine and, by extension, their ability to heal with spiritual light.

- TYR – The Spiritual Warrior as Shaman.
- BJARKA – as the healer, herbalist, host of rites of passage work etc. BARKA definitely is a "shaman".
- EH = The Psychopomp, Soul Conductor, Horse Shaman.
- MADR = The part of us which stays in communication with ancestors.
- LAGU: Water is a tremendous healer and shapeshifter. It nourishes all new life forms. It gives us blood and sacred tears. It is often used in spiritual cleansing.
- ING: Shamans plants the seeds of a new paradigm.
- ODAL is not a shaman but definitely a temple, an enclosed sacred space.
- DAGAZ represents enlightenment. Shamans bring altered states of consciousness and illumination.
- FE: The cattle herder as animal communicator. "The Lord is my Shepherd" (Bible).

Hag Runes

As I grow older and embrace life as a Hag and Elder, I have also meditated on where the Hag (or power of the wise crone) appears in the runes:

- As UR She represents the undivided untamed principle of primordial femininity, her rune is the womb of the goddess.
- At THURS the Goddess meets her Other, the male god as a consort.
- ASS is the male God, fertilising principle and sacred masculine force, Consort of UR.

- REID: People used to pull wagons across the land in fertility rites (so gifts and abundance of GIFU will occur).
- At KEN She is primordial creativity, the Mysterious Mother of both Shaman and Blacksmith. (She trains her children and has her own forge).
- GIFU: the sacred marriage of the Goddess of the Land to the King (ruler of the Earth Realm) occurs, also the marriage of Nerthus (UR) and Freyr (ASS). The Pregnant Hag is all ages and all stages between seed and Hag.
- WYNJA is seedbed of wedded bliss (for the figures mentioned above).
- HAGAL: Fertility is done for this year. The Goddess grows into her Crone Self. The Grandmother Activist does not shy away from drastic action and world changing events. She risks her own life to protect young life. She knows her way to the Underworld and back. The Hag sits on the fence, which separates the village from the wilderness. We meet her as the Fence or Gate (Heth), our 8th letter, when the soul enters the wilderness of the Underworld through the Gate that is HAGAL.
- NAUD: The Hag in her manifestation as the Mother of Necessity. When the birds start migrating, rune ALGIZ becomes the footprint of the Crane-Crone. As the Mother of the Dying Year, she opens her womb to returning souls, released from their mortal coil. Death releases us from (linear) Earth time. Growing grain ends with both a harvest and the harvest of souls.
- IS is the Hag as the Ice Bridge, fearless clarity, the road to Niflhel.
- JARA: The Hag as the provider of abundance and food for all beings. Long before Jesus she knew she had to die on behalf of her community.

- PERTHRA: The Hag as the Mountain Mother, the womb-tomb goddess, as above so below: within her rocky womb we find the starry sky, the entire universe.
- EOH: The Hag is the spindle or axis mundi around which the seasons turn. She is Frigg, she is Mother Holle, she is the Elder Tree.
- ALGIZ: The Hag as the Mother of Animals and Mistress of Game, also Forest Mother (Finnish Mielikki). Algiz is the footprint of the Crane-Crone.
- SOL: As the mysterious figure of Sinthgunt the Hag is a Sister of the Sun/Sunna. Both know about cycles and chanting healing charms.
- TYR: The arrow = also an upside-down spindle. This represents the connection of the Hag to spinning and weaving, her Frau Holle manifestation, also PERCHTA – PERTHRA.
- BJARKA: The Hag as Birch Mother who overseas rites of passage for younger women.
- EH: The Hag in her manifestation of Otherworld Horse Goddess (think of the Celtic Epona and Rhiannon).
- MADR: The Hag as the Mother of Mankind and Earth as our Primordial Ancestor.
- LAGU: The Hag as Lady of the Lake and Mother Water.
- ING: The Hag as the safe container for fertility and the fertilising principle.
- ODAL = The Hag as a safe enclosure where entry must be earned, the Mistress of Home and Hearth.
- DAGAZ = The Hag is both total darkness and blinding light, the Illuminatrix.
- FE = the Hag in her manifestation of cattle herder and Primordial Cow. This is Holy Cow of India, before she turns feral and reappears as UR.

Hyperborea (a runic rabbit hole)

> The North is not just a compass point but a state of mind
> -Christopher McIntosh[1]

As part of the research for this book I went down a rabbit hole researching Hyperborea and the notion of Hyperborean runes. Instead of covering this material I direct you to the work of Christopher McIntosh.

A Fear of the Runes

Is history fated to repeat itself? A student from Germany once told me that her friends had told her to stop studying the runes, because they are "Nazi symbols". You cannot study material from the Northern Tradition without a painful awareness of the way that the Nazis twisted and abused some of this material, in their efforts to inflict harm on a scale that defies the human imagination.

Some people make the argument that this body of material (including the runes) is so tainted that we had better walk away from it altogether. I recently listened to a (generally high quality) podcast where the runes were casually dismissed as "Nazi symbols". This is upsetting. It is my conviction that the Northern Tradition *especially* needs people with integrity, practicing and teaching this material correctly and authentically.

Teaching with a focus on historical accuracy includes educating people about how Nazis twisted the material. In an ideal situation groups of rune magicians in our time would work together diligently to eradicate this stain (in other worlds, dispel it on an energetic level). Most of our rune magician ancestors left a positive "footprint", not a crime scene!

Forensic Science: The Runes as Detectives

In 2023 I taught an experimental class to test my conviction that the runes can be used to solve crimes, or long-standing mysteries. Our group focussed on one famous mystery (which was probably a crime but remains unsolved until today).

All my students worked in different ways and they often contributed a different set of core meanings to a given rune (compared to what I had taught them). Nevertheless, I mapped all information. A pattern of intersecting circles, resembling a complex Venn diagram, appeared on my notepad. A fairly consistent picture emerged of what had happened.

Please do not get me wrong. I would never claim that a rune magician working alone can solve any crime or mystery on our planet. I am just saying that skillful use of runes, by an experienced group of people, can add another lens of perception, another way of interpreting patterns and clusters, *useful information.*

Shadow Work

By all means read grimoires, make sigils and start a Book of Shadows (a personal record of spells, beliefs, pathworkings and magical workings) but any self-respecting rune magician needs to do shadow work, fearless daily inner work. Many people want to have more power but only few are willing to reflect deeply on the wide range of possibilities for abuse that having more power brings. You will find two book recommendations in the *Recommended Reading List (Appendix).*

Blóts

In the Viking Age (about 800–1050 CE) Blóts (sacrificing or offering ceremonies) were organised at regular intervals to perform divination. We know this from words such as *blót-spánn* (rods or chips used for divination) and *dreyr-stafir* (bloody staves or falling staves). We know that lots were cast to consult the gods (*Germania, Vita Willibrordi, Vita Ansgari*). The Old Norse word *blót-fé* means 'enchanted object' denoting at one time something sacred and sometimes something "cursed". It signifies a spirit-possessed object. *Blóts* were even performed to achieve desired outcomes in legal matters: "investing in the right outcome".[2] The description above explains the (origin of the) tradition you are stepping into, but I encourage you to work in ways to suit the sensibilities of modern times.

A (controversial) Closing Reflection

Decades of spiritual work has taught me that *we can call things into being*. Words or names can be like vessels or containers and, given the opportunity, spirit will fill the containers we create. I sometimes liken this to an employment agency: by asking for help, we create "jobs" that certain spirits can fill. This furthers the evolution of consciousness which happens in mutually beneficial spirit-human partnerships (EH).

We can create our own system and assign meaning to (any) objects. The spirits will engage with the meanings we assign, even if our system has no historical accuracy. This is mind-boggling but it opens vast reservoirs of meaning and potential.

Rune magician students taking their first baby steps are often surprised that there is no Moon rune or child rune etc. I hope that this book has demonstrated how we find the entire universe: all deities, concepts and historical periods within the runes, if only we know where to look.

A sigil for protection

Part II

Threads of Fate
(Ørlǫgþátto)

A Compendium of Runic Axes

Part II of this book can be used while runes are pulled (for yourself or others) and also when more complex rune readings or workings are performed. It will give you themes to be alert to, and provide additional dimensions (themes and storylines) to explore.

I have primarily used Old Norse sources but I have also dipped into world mythology, to show that we are encountering universal patterns or blueprints (and to provide the closest matches for the dynamics described).

This is a *reference section,* intended to be used the same way that a (hard copy) dictionary is used. It does not have standard chapters, but all rune axes are listed by the first rune (following the UTHARK order, therefore assigning first place to Rune UR, second place to Rune THURS and so forth) of any pair.

Every axis is listed only once. Therefore: *I have not made a distinction between KEN – LAGU and LAGU – KEN, so you need to locate it by following the rune sequence. KEN appears before LAGU, so find this axis under KEN.* However, one could arrive at subtle distinctions, if one considers the first rune to be more dominant than the second. Track and report back please!

This section also references material from folklore and ancestral European witchcraft traditions (not Wicca). It is important to note that Christianity merged earlier references to "The Old One" (an ancient chthonic deity, who was the protector of secret knowledge, medicine, magic and fertility) with the Christian "Devil". They are not the same being and it is important not to confuse them. Radomir Ristic explains that the Devil does exist in Balkan Craft but he is a completely different character from Satan. In some Serbian traditions *the Devil is the deadly enemy of Satan.*[1]

Good rune magicians are life-long students, always asking questions and learning.

UR

Fertile chaos, wild untamed power, a void teeming with potentialities.

UR – THURS = The Self-Other Axis and Othering
Fear lives on the Edge of the Wilderness. – Corinne Boyer[2] This is the axis of separation and individuation. "Thorny" Rune THURS takes us back to a primal moment: the corruption or interruption of Divine Unity at birth, when our umbilical cord is cut. Number two brings duality and twins. It also creates couples because human beings desire a mate. Note from my rune journal: *the hunger for darkness is the yearning to be back in the cauldron of UR.*

UR – ASS = Cosmogony
The Void (UR) birthed Divine Consciousness and elementary forces. Some of those powers evolved into deities. Humans have innate divinity, an ensouling divine spark.

UR – REID = The Birth of Movement
Events are set in motion. The wheel of karma starts spinning. The circle of the runes keeps turning too. Movement brings time, cycles, movement, chronology, continuity, stories and music.

UR – KEN = The Divine Blacksmith
Blacksmiths forge both tools and weapons. The latter connects blacksmiths to malevolence, crime and warfare. Communities both *need and fear* their blacksmiths. Folklore speaks of blacksmiths making a pact with the Devil to gain supernatural power.

UR – GIFU = The Gift of Life and Gefjon's Oxen
Gefjon travelled through Sweden, disguised as a homeless woman. King Gylfi granted her as much land "as four oxen could plow in one day". Gefjon summoned her four sons (fathered by an unnamed giant), and turned them into oxen. They plowed the land, but they also dragged it down to Denmark. The resulting hollow space became Lake Mälaren. The scooped-out earth became the Danish island of Zealand, where Copenhagen is situated.

UR – WYNJA = Primal Joy and Being in Flow
Here we follow our bliss and we experience a primal creative force expressing itself through us. When we are *in flow,* doubts, anxieties and other preoccupations drop away. We lose track of time. We merge with powers greater than ourselves.

UR – HAGAL = HAGAL as UR-Mother and Uber-Witch
Rune magicians think of HAGAL, written in the form of a six-pointed star (from which a web-like grid can be created) as the *Mother of All Runes*. This makes HAGAL a primordial mother. HAGAL is also the rune of witches. Sudden catastrophic change is a divine intervention of the Primordial Hag!

UR – NAUD = The Mother of Necessity
The Primordial Mother becomes the *Mother of Necessity*. Her children are her greatest joy. Her greatest sorrow is that she must impose death of them, to give all her children a go at life.

UR – IS = Where Audhumbla Licks Buri out of the Ice
Awakening from dormancy occurs here. In the Nordic region ice is a formidable force. It offers both danger and opportunities (hypothermia and traveling long distances over ice). Internally, Ice acts as a mirror for our soul.

UR – JARA = Fjǫrgyn as Mother Earth
Fjǫrgyn is sometimes equated with Jord as Earth. She represents the Life-Giving Principle becoming manifest reality on Earth. Mother Earth provides for us, by means of the harvest.

UR – PERTHRA = The Primordial Mountain Mother
PERTHRA is the rune of rocks and mountains. Her indwelling spirit is the Mountain Mother, who presides over rocks, caves and all mountain ranges.

UR – EOH = The First Tree and the Placenta
Here we observe bison retreating into the depths of the great Hercynian Forest) that once covered much of ancient "Germania".[3]

UR – ALGIZ = The Primal Familiar or our Wild Twin
Rewilding and Wildness as a Foreign Power[4]
We learn how to make a distinction between what is wild or feral, what needs re-wilding and what is completely beyond our control. Martin Shaw wrote a book titled *Courting the Wild Twin*. This Wild Twin represents the part of us which remains connected to both Earth and Nature (SW Jord) but also our own nature: raw emotion and expression, things that are socialized out of us at a young age and become "repressed". We can regain vitality by courting our Wild Twin.[5]

UR – SOL = Sunna as the Primordial Light-Giving Principle
The Sun is perceived as a female giantess in Norse cosmology and the Moon *(Máni)* as her brother. Astronomically speaking she is a star: a hot glowing ball of gas. She represents the principle of giving (GIFU) because she is slowly burning out, while providing light and heat.

UR – TYR = The Axis of the Primordial Warrior

Shamanic work with veterans led me to the book "War and Soul" by Edward Tick. I learned that war, and the archetype of the warrior, are deeply wired into the human psyche. We cannot eradicate it, but we can use our awareness to manifest this urge or drive in a higher manifestation.

UR – BJARKA = The Axis of Mother Birch

Birch is a pioneer tree, the first tree to grow in Scandinavia after the Ice Age receded. It is also the first tree to grow on disturbed land (after logging or forest fires etc.)

UR – EH = The Great Cycle of Life-Death-Rebirth

This axis charts our cosmic origin (and the birth of our world or universe). It describes life and death on Earth. Ultimately it maps the return to unity consciousness. Life and Death are like Yin and Yang, where Life contains the Seed of Death just as Death contains the Seed of Life. Life and Death are sacred twins.

UR – MADR = Survival

The Interface Between Human Beings and Wildness

Aboriginal or Indigenous Peoples

Extinct Peoples who Live on in our Ancestral Field as Deep Ancestors

We create human-made environments where we (try to) control every aspect of life, from air-conditioning and medical interventions to high-rise cities teeming with people. Yet, *"The Wild" still meets us everywhere:* deep within ourselves, in other people's unpredictability and actions, the dangers of urban jungles, the predators of the online dating world and at vulnerable times (loss, illness, pregnancy, injury etc.)

UR – LAGU = Watery Primeval Chaos
Sleep And Dreaming
All Life-Supporting Fluids

I took up wild swimming last summer. A seasoned *wild swimmer,* had told me about the powerful surges and currents that occur in the sea: you cannot control them, so you need to be extremely mindful of personal safety. Here we also find all life-supporting fluids: amniotic fluid, blood, semen, breast milk etc. Audhumla (probably) suckled Ymir.

UR – ING

This axis is about Life's longing for itself, for the continuation of Life *at all cost, or* under any circumstances. Birth is a forceful (almost "violent") physical process and (post-partum trauma and depression exist for a reason). Many children on our planet are born into circumstances that do not even meet basic human rights. Yet, Life insists on continuing.

UR – ODAL = Ancestral Home
Our Sense Of Belonging On Earth

We need to belong and feel that our life has meaning in the larger weave or tapestry of humanity. The Latin word *religare* (from which our word religion is derived) means "to bind back". This axis is our umbilical cord to Spirit, as we conceptualise it in our cosmology of choice.

UR – DAGAZ = The Axis Of Enlightenment

This axis is about casting light on things, a new perspective, shifting to a more enlightened state of consciousness. The New Age has brought a tendency for people to focus exclusively on the benevolent side of spirituality: angels, compassionate ancestors, helpful deities etc. This leaves people with an impoverished spiritual toolkit, which can lead to spiritual narcissism.[6] Note from my rune journal:

the centre of Rune DAGAZ is the Void space, which opens and expands into UR.

UR – FE = The Gjallarhorn
The Oscillation Between Feral Aurochs and Domesticated Cattle

Heimdallr guards Bifrost and will blow his gjallarhorn (UR – FE) when Ragnarok starts.

Civilizations end. The Stock Market crashes. FE marks a point of completion, but "full circle" often invites another start, another round of something. AI and how it will change our society completely is a hot issue. There are fears of unleashing something that cannot be controlled or rolled back. Several AI experts say that AI may just decide that the elimination of all human beings is the best way to save our planet. In a sense we all live under "the cloud of Ragnarok".

THURS or THURISAZ

Thor, the Thursar ("giants"), thorn.

THURS – ASS = Trickster and Dualistic Deity
The Primordial Scream and Wounding Words
A Double Life, Living a Lie

P.R. Woodruff writes that all female and male Slavic deities have an opposite-sex consort. In this divine relationship of a god and goddess they are lovers. At the same time, they are twin brother and sister, generated by one divine dual-sex being. Knowing this we can go in search of lost deities.[7]

THURS – REID: Circles, Cycles and Stories
Trauma as Time Travel
Road Rage

Unresolved karmic wounds in the human psyche appear to drive incarnation. Healing often expresses itself through efforts to balance the scales. Wounded people keep on re-creating a core trauma, in an unconscious attempt to learn, heal and resolve. Because they do so unconsciously, most of the time there is no resolution, only repetition. Painful experiences in a human life will also cause us to draw conclusions which shape future experiences. On this axis we need to change the script.

THURS – KEN = The Art of Deception
Weapons and Warfare
Our Immune System
The blacksmith is often depicted as lame. In many old myths, physical defects are linked to divinity and god-like powers. But those people also served as a reminder that God would punish those who aspired to possess Divine knowledge. Shamans are called (often against their will) to channel and harness this power while others are struck down for actively seeking this path. *Rune KEN is a pine torch which can illuminate both sides of thorny matters we find at THURS.*

THURS – GIFU = Finding the Gift in Adversity
The Illness as the Cure (Paradox)
Hallowing or Cursing
Deceit: Thor Disguised as a Bride
The role of the archetypal Trickster (Loki or mercurial Odin) is to straddle two sides without splitting themselves. Instead, they split a situation, family or community instead. We all know people who play this role, in real life. For indigenous people the concepts of a "good" god and "evil" god makes as much sense as a "good" fire or "evil" fire. They just are, but you would want to protect yourself from any unwanted effects.[8]

THURS – WYNJA = Choosing Your Battles and Keeping the Peace

WYNJA brings joy but THURS brings conflict. Choose your battles! Ask yourself: "Is this the hill I am willing to die on?"

THURS – HAGAL = The Witch Wound

Trauma – Initiation

The Witch Wound starts with Gullveig. In the Vǫluspá, she came to the hall of Odin and is speared by the Æsir, burnt three times, yet reborn three times. Upon her third rebirth, she began practicing seiðr and took the name Heiðr (bright). Many scholars believe that she is Freyja. On the Initiation – Trauma axis, a rip occurs in the fabric of everyday reality. We are catapulted into the Unknown. The difference between THURS and HAGAL is that HAGAL gives us no choice. At THURS we can choose the forge and a baptism of fire, or walk away. Curses and cursing belong here too. Both blackthorn and thorny THURS runes are used in transgressive magical operations, where "evil fights evil".

THURS – NAUD = The Twisted Barb of Fate

Dire necessity is embedded in medicine. Being wounded or ill makes us do counter-intuitive things in our quest for healing: we eat poison plants, accept radiation and yield to chemotherapy. There is an intrinsic link between duality and healing. When an imbalance occurs, the cure is often found in its opposite or counterpart.

THURS – IS = Skaði, Niflheim and the Frost Giants

Frozen Emotions and Projections

The giants (literally "devourers") are chaos-bringers, and the North is the direction of Death. Skaði is the winter goddess and embodies all these things. When serious trauma occurs, human beings freeze, fight, flight or fawn. Trauma freezes parts of us and/or our perception (of others) freezes too. Trauma stops time.

THURS – JARA = Pandora's Box
Going Against the Grain
The Devil's Acre or Lone Acre
Cancel Culture

Here we find things that *go against the grain*. Those brave enough to do so are demonized or "cancelled". They end up carrying the shadows of others (and in more extreme or high-profile cases the shadows of the collective). We used to call this phenomenon witch hunts.

THURS – PERTHRA = Mjolnir

The motion of Mjolnir, Thor's hammer, resembles a lightning bolt. In an older, Germanic, version of this myth, his hammer was made of stone. It was not (yet) the iron weapon forged by the *Svartálfar* (black elves) and dwarfs Sindri and Brokkr.[9] Mjolnir unfailingly returns, much like a boomerang.

THURS – EOH = The Relationship Between Thor And Ullr
The Hercynian Forest

This axis flags thorny and poisonous trees, especially the toxicity of yew trees. Some sources claim that Ullr is the stepson of Thor, because Thor's wife (Sif) is his mother. Ullr is associated with the yew tree and his domain is called Ydalir (Yew Dales). This would link thorny trees and bushes) to the yew tree.

THURS – Algiz = The Exorcist
The Relationship Between Animals and Humans
The Wild Adversary or Lord of Wild Places
The Old King of Witches

Fear lives on the edge of Wildness.[10]

To release ourselves from the iron gloves of darkness (ignorance and lack of self-awareness), we need to connect to our innate wildness. We need to unravel scripts of acculturation and socialisation, to regain the ability to think independently.

Human beings need to walk a fine line between herd behaviour and independent critical thinking. I think that the way we treat animals (not pets) will, one day, be viewed with the same disapproval, verging on disbelief, as Western society now feels about slavery.

THURS – SOL = The Pathway Lightning Takes
Refraction and Fractals

Lightning brings light, a brief flash of illumination. *Was there lightning (striking the primordial waters) before there was light? Lightning can illuminate and damage or injure.* This is also the axis of light breaking up into colours or patterns. In physics, *refraction* is the redirection of a wave as it passes from one medium to another and a fractal is self-repeating pattern.

THURS – TYR = Fight Or Flight

Thor is always fighting giants while Tyr sacrifices a hand or arm to the Fenris Wolf, to keep Ragnarok at bay. The *fight-or-flight* response refers to a physiological reaction that occurs in the presence of something that is terrifying. These were the choices our ancestors had when faced with danger.

THURS – BJARKA = The Poison Mother, Dark Mother or Shadow Mother
Thor's Mother
Acupuncture

Every rune has a bright side and a shadow side. Here lives the inversion, or shadow of BJARKA, where medicine turns back to poison and maternal love turns possessive and domineering. This is also the mother who will resort to violence to protect her children. In the fairytale about Sleeping Beauty, a 13th uninvited guest at her birth, often referred to as a wicked godmother, predicts that the princess will die when she pricks her finger on a spindle. Her parents clear the entire kingdom of spindles, but the prophecy (or curse) still comes true with one difference: the princess falls into a deep sleep instead, until a prince wakes her up.

THURS – EH = Ymir and Yama
The First Twins: Life and Death
The Deceased as "Other"
The Dead Perceived as Corrupting Influences

The primordial giant Ymir was dismembered by the gods. Our world was created from the body parts. In the Vedic texts we meet Ymir as Yama: the *Receiver of Souls*. The first being to die becomes the Lord of the Dead and welcomes all those who die after him.[11] There were elaborate rituals for moving a corpse from their home to the churchyard. This protected the living from danger or "corruption".

THURS – MADR = Where We Meet the Other in the Flesh
Herd Immunity
The Human Predator

Passing through the sharpened hedge into the Devil's terrain requires the ability to withstand the painful process of exposing vulnerable places, risking wound and scar that could very well occur with intimate contact…[12] This axis maps a very complex territory because it represents human consciousness evolving through "thorny experiences". It is the axis of projection, gaslighting and scapegoating.

THURS – LAGU = The Potion – Poison Axis
Well-Poisoners
Trickster and Reversal Medicine
Sexually Transmitted Diseases

Human beings depend on water sources. Wells are sometimes poisoned as a warfare strategy, but well-poisoner is also a term for people in a workplace with a poor attitude and bad influence over others. They tend to contaminate their environment with negative and unsafe behaviour.[13]

THURS – ING = Sowing Wild Oats
The Seed of Duality
Poison Plant Seeds

On this axis harmful events are "seeded". Crimes and terrorist attacks all start with a seed concept. There is also some ambiguity here: good things can come out of bad situations and good intentions can misfire.

THURS – ODAL = Our Home as a Sanctuary
"Hausfriede" (German for a Peaceful Home)
Foreign Countries
Even Demons Demand Their Shrine
Allowing Ancestral Land to Rewild Itself
The Word "Outlandish"

In Old Germanic law, any building is inviolable (*Hausfriede, safe and sacred private space*) and no one could pursue a malefactor into the latter's own house or that of his neighbour. Whoever broke this law was sentenced to capital punishment.[14] In our day the media report tragic incidents where someone experienced a home invasion (US term) and used "too much force or violence" to defend themselves or protect their family. Stories about such people ending up in prison evoke a profound sense of injustice in most of us. The older law still echoes in our ancestral soul.

THURS – DAGAZ = The Dark Twin Enlightens Us

There is an immense tendency in our culture for "spiritual people" to focus only on the benevolent side of spiritual practices and deities. Mythology teaches us unequivocally that there are wrathful deities too (or more accurately, that all deities have both benevolent and destructive manifestations). Violence forever seeks creative new expressions and outlets:

violent computer games with a "kill score", date rapes through dating apps (where sex is essentially expected on the first date), bullying on Instagram etc. The opposite is happening too: micro-aggressions, non-hate hate crimes, *deadnaming,* and demands for *safe spaces* by privileged university students.

THURS – FE
Threat or harm to cattle and livestock. In our day: threats to our wealth and prosperity.

ASS

God Rune, God Force, Divine Speech, ecstatic work.

ASS – REID = The Prime Mover and Mythic Time
Career Progress
Astrology and Horoscopes
Myth Weavers
Adhd and AI
The Prime Mover sets everything in motion. Time and movement are twinned. Everything cyclical and circular is found here.

"Every construction is a creation, a beginning, the reiteration of a mythical act, a cosmogony, and therefore requires precise rites so that it confirms to the archetype."[15] Some minds move too fast: we currently see a proliferation of ADHD. Arguably iPhones and screens promote or increase this. People can also become possessed by a myth, idea or archetype. Their ideas run away with them. Related phenomena are cults, brainwashing and way-out conspiracy theories. This is also the axis of Artificial Intelligence.

ASS – KEN = Torch-Bearers and Fire Thieves
Our Fetter to Spirit

Human beings need an umbilical cord to Spirit or powers greater than themselves. We need to be in service to a greater good and other people. That is the fetter forged on this axis.

ASS – GIFU = The Hieros Gamos (Sacred Marriage)
Ecstasy and Altered States of Consciousness
Crossroads Where Humans Meet Deities

This axis describes the blessings and reciprocity brought by interaction between deities and human beings. We build religions, belief systems and cosmologies. Human marriages on Earth reflect themes from of marriages between deities.

ASS – WYNJA = Divine Ecstasy, Bliss

This is the axis of spirit work or deity work. The word ecstasy literally means "standing outside ourselves". Frigg can be described as the Midwife of Unity Consciousness, as a deity of home and hearth, a bringer of harmony and reconciliation.

ASS – HAGAL = The Crone Goddess as Deified Witch
Witches Causing (Hail) Storms

Everything involving pure witchcraft forbids any kind of clear speech. Although witches used dancing [REID –HAGAL IA] to achieve a state of trance, they were not allowed to speak, but performed their rituals in silence.[16] HAGAL is the Queen (or Mother) of Witches. On this axis we encounter or master the specials powers of witches.

ASS – NAUD = The Power of the Norns & Hubris

The sources state clearly that the Norns are more powerful than the gods. They carve the fate of all beings, *including* the gods. This is also the axis of *hubris*: human beings or deities pitting themselves against their "fated limits" and wreaking havoc on their own lives and the lives of others.

ASS – IS = Grandfather Frost
Ice as an Elemental Deity
Languages of the Ice Age

Here we meet the frost giants and Skaði on her skis. In Russia Grandfather Frost is called Ded Moroz. In English we speak of Jack Frost. The ancient Indians worshipped the elements as deities. I am fascinated by the (long lost) languages people spoke during the Ice Age. Research demonstrates that some words from those languages live on in modern languages. Note from my rune journal: *Did Grandfather Frost marry Grandmother Fire?*

ASS – JARA = The Harvest Queen or Deity

At Delphi the priestess began her formal ritual address to the gods as follows:

> *"First in my prayer before all other gods,*
> *I call on Earth, primeval prophetess"*
> (Gaia was at Delphi long before Apollo)[17]

ASS – PERTHRA = Stones as the Bones Of Mother Earth
The Cave as a Womb
The Son of the Mountain Mother

Caves and caverns are liminal places, portals to the underworld or other worlds. Cities have underworlds too: London has underground rivers and abandoned underground stations. During Cave Time we replenish our inner world and meet a motley crew of mythical characters.

ASS – EOH = Odin's Ordeal on the Windswept Tree
The Family Tree of Gods
Wood Wind Instruments
Hercynia

Once upon a time dense woods (called Hercynia by the Romans) covered much of Germanic Europe. Much of the land was cleared and the tree deities retreated. After their demotion, they turned into the imps and spirits of folklore.[18] We still hear their voices in woodwind instruments...

ASS – EOH = Displaced Ancient Deities Finding Sanctuary in Wild Woods

The old gods endured much longer on this wooded fringe of Europe than they did elsewhere.[19] Gaining divine knowledge involves ordeals and sacrifices. To call back old (or forgotten) gods, we must venerate them and give them wild spaces: sanctuaries and outdoor temples.

ASS – ALGIZ = The Horned or Antlered God
Deified Wild Creatures
Divine Protection
"Director of Dances of the Gods"

"O God, Beast, Mystery, come!"[20] Our ancestors understood that forests had their own goddesses and gods. In Finland we find Tapio and Mielikki. In Sweden we have the Skogsrå. Medeinė is a Lithuanian forest goddess. Latvian folklore has both a "forest mother" and "forest father," as well as a "mother of shrubs."[21] The real name of a deity was too holy to use on a regular basis, so titles or descriptions were used instead. Bear was a prime example in Northern Europe and Russia. People spoke of *The Old Man of the Forest, Honey Paws* or *Grandpa in his fur coat* etc. Modern culture lacks this reverence. Trees and body parts of animals are used to make musical instruments. Horsehair was used as strings for violins. I have two swan bone flutes.

ASS – SOL = SUNNA

Scandinavian petroglyphs show that Sunna (the Sun) was a primary deity of the Bronze Age, meaning that she is much older than the Norse gods as we know them today. Scholars suggest that Sól, as a goddess, may well represent an extension of an earlier Proto-Indo-European deity.[22]

ASS – TYR = Incantations and Oaths
The Spiritual Warrior

Tyr is not a personal name, the word means god. Tyr is the rune of one-handed spiritual warrior. We moderns have eternity or infinite rings (symbolizing never-ending love).[23] Old Norse people had oath rings. The Vikings saw them as a symbol of reciprocity and commitment. A man or woman's word was binding, and any person of merit would sooner die than break a promise. We moderns strive to be "good" people. The Old Norse people were concerned with being "honourable" people.

ASS – BJARKA = The Divine Mother
Birch Tree Spirit and Female Pioneer
Magical Charms and Incantations

The Slavic Goddess Mara is a Protector of Mothers and Daughters. On this axis we move from pure god force to 'divine power in action': galdr and magical charms, incantations, the Bards and Skalds. The Norse had a rich oral tradition and "song-smiths".

ASS – EH = The Kiss of Death
The Wild Hunt
Necromancy

On this axis Life and Death embrace (and kiss) as sacred lovers. Death is the flip side of sex and procreation (life-giving activities). To understand the dynamics of this axis I listened to some interviews with serial killers. One described killing as "doing what you love most, seeing the very atoms of Creation vibrate". Ted Bundy went one step further and called himself

"God" or "The Master of the Universe", in the moment of strangling and killing a woman. Horrifyingly, there is a god-like power in killing and ending a life.[24]

ASS – MADR = Innate Divinity
Divine Ancestors
Seeing the Divinity Behind the Symbols

> *"Strive not thou to become a god, the things of mortals best become mortality."*
> -Pindar[25]

Human beings can connect to gods because they possess an innate divinity of their own. The dedicated followers of deities (priests, priestesses, shamans, druids or witches etc.) often bear the name of the god(dess) they are connected to. The Slavic goddess Mora had "fairy moras", who belonged to her domain. Any witch followers would also be called moras. Striga has the eerie fey *strzyga* or *strix,* (which have gotten maligned through the years), and Veles has the *vile (veela).*[26] In the Swedish province of Östergötland we find a (small) mountain called Omberget. Local folklore tells us this mountain has its own goddess. Over the centuries there has been a lineage of priestesses in her service, but they all look the same because they wear an owl mask.

PLW offers us five distinct blueprints (or archetypal imprints) for spirit work[27]:

- The Mystic who transcends the self in relationship to the Divine
- The Martyr who sacrifices the self for a cause or another
- The Savior who forgets the self for the sake of another

- The Victim who loses the self at the mercy of another
- The Madman whose conscious self is overcome by the contents of his subconscious

These archetypes are not set for life. As we evolve and rewrite our scripts, we often move steadily closer to The Mystic. We grow wise.

ASS – LAGU = Water Deities and the Nine Wave Maidens

Rán is the Norse goddess of the Sea. Her name means robbery. She represents the dangerous, treacherous and harsh aspects of the sea. She is married to Aegir who brews ale in his cauldron and hosts feasts for the gods. Aegir is a god of the deep sea; he *is* the sea! They have nine daughters: the Wave Maidens. Njord (Njǫrðr) is a sea deity too, but a Vanir god and associated with coastal waters and the sea as a source of food for human beings. In its negative manifestation this is the axis of intoxication and communing with the wrong kind of "spirits".

ASS – ING = The God of the Seedpod

Seed Power

The Sexuality and Infidelity of the Gods

ING is the rune of the god Freyr, perceived as both a seed and a storehouse of potential. Freyr is the twin brother of Freyja. Seeds must scatter widely. Only some will take root and become plants.

ASS – ODAL = House Gods

The Halls of the Norse Gods

Our Home is Our Temple

Most Norse gods have their own halls or domains in other worlds. Few modern people live in (or have access to) an ancestral homestead. When a farm consisted of just a single building that was at once a dwelling, stable, cowshed, pigsty, hayloft and granary, there was only one household spirit. When the farm consisted of a dwelling house and dependent buildings, we find specialized spirits for each structure.[28] A house is much more than a building. It is a microcosm, a living being with both a body and soul. It speaks, even if its language is only creaking and cracking noises for the profane.[29]

ASS – DAGAZ = Enlightenment
Alternating Gods Dividing up the Year

Working with deities raises our consciousness and provides a higher perspective. The gods evolve too, in partnership with human beings. We see the evolution of deities in the way that they have "sons and daughters" and branch off. (Nerthus became Frigg and Freyja). In many locations deities are also connected to seasons and the lifestyle of humans (e.g. hunter-gatherers or farmers). The Old Norse people only knew two seasons: *skammdegi* (short days, winter) and *nóttleysa* (nightless period, summer). *Deities are not bound by any mortal form. They can appear in many different guises. Originally there was no "mother" or "father" of a pantheon with a "supreme god". The lore of gods "fighting each other" for dominance comes from warrior culture. Those are recent human constructs.*[30]

ASS – FE = The Sacred Cow
Cow Goddesses
Wind Instruments made from Body Parts of Animals

Here we find the divinity (or divine manifestation) of animals and cow goddesses. We also find wind instruments and the sacred gift of music. In the Kalavala, the Finnish god Väinämöinen seats himself *on a hill all silver shining* and lures the wolves out of their lairs, the fish out of the rivers and the birds out of the branches.[31]

REID

Riding, wheels, the wagons of the gods.

REID – KEN = Blacksmiths Keep Wheels Turning And Wagons Rolling

Rhythm And Repetition

It could be argued that REID is the Rune of Astrology, as the "the science of interpreting cosmic or celestial patterning". It is also the study of frequence and vibration. What goes around comes around. At REID we find rhythm and repetition. Rune KEN asks: Was the Prime Mover a divine blacksmith? The Dwarfs forged power tools for some Norse Gods:

- *Mjolnir*: Thor's hammer (which moves: it returns to Thor after being thrown, like a boomerang)
- *Skíðblaðnir:* a ship belonging to Freyr that always has a favourable wind (movement)
- *Draupnir*: Odin's ring would drip eight new rings every ninth night (more circles or wheels)
- *Gungnir*: Odin's spear would hit its target without fail (movement)

REID – GIFU = The Karmic Gift or (Energy) Exchange

Here we meet GIFU as the "patron rune" for travellers". *Paying it forward* is an excellent motto for this axis. We can also learn from the experiences of others. Perhaps history is not bound to repeat itself?

REID – WYNJA = The Joys of Travel

Soothing Repetition

This is the joy of a healthy body with healthy cycles and circadian rhythms.

Travel remains a growth industry. Repetition and predictability can be reassuring, even soothing. Stimming is a means of self-soothing for people on the autistic spectrum.

REID – HAGAL = Cosmic Repetition
The Witch as Storyteller and Teacher
Wayfaring Witches

Cataclysmic disaster visits at regular intervals to fertilise and destabilize the course of history and brings *Change (with a capital letter C).* Witches were known to fly around in egg shells.[32] Serbian witches used dancing to achieve a state of altered consciousness.[33]

REID – NAUD = Ørlǫg
The Norns Apportioning the Life Span of all Beings

The Old Norse word Ørlǫg means primal law: "what is carved or fated". It refers to shaping forces and immutable characteristics: genetic material, parents and location of birth, (dis)abilities and talents. Ørlǫg is not personal, it just *is*. Rune NAUD refers to the necessity to roll with what we have.

REID – IS = Doing Versus Being
The Eye of the Storm
Deep Time
Glacial Archeology
Glaciers as Portals to the Ice Ages[34]

Here we move from Doing to Being. This is the axis of "mindfulness and letting Life whirl all around us" without being sucked into any vortex. This is a paradox: there is motion in stillness and stillness at the heart of a hurricane. History thaws. Due to global warming ice is melting in many locations. Artifacts and biological specimens, preserved by freezing temperatures, are surfacing at sites as diverse as Paleo-Eskimo middens in Greenland, burials in the Altai Mountains of Russia and mummies of the Andes.[35]

REID – JARA = Harvesting

The Plough as a Revolving Wheel

The harvest is the completion of a successful growing cycle. But any harvest also sits in a long succession of previous or ancestral harvests (which helped our ancestors survive). In Lithuania the Slavic god Radagast was called *Radagais,* meaning "The Revolving Wheel" (a suitable name for a sun god linked to ploughing).[36]

REID – PERTRHA = Storied Stone and Stone Circles

"Skeppsättningar" (Standing Stones in Ship Formation)

All Things Megalithic

On this axis we find standing stones, stone circles (or stone ships, SW *skeppsättningar*) and all the mysteries surrounding them. Especially aspects (or theories) related to calendars, timekeeping and seasons, Stone Age astronomy. Were stone circles "astronomical computers"?

REID – EOH = Axial Precession, Markers of Time and Axis Mundi

The Axis Mundi Around Which the World Spins

Yggdrasil, the world tree, can be viewed as the rotational axis (or spine) around which the world spins. It has been suggested that standing stones are markers in the landscape of a solar year. The markers of Time (sticks and towers casting shadows) slowly become inaccurate over large periods of time due to axial precession (a gravity-induced and slow, but continuous change in where Earth's axis points).

REID – ALGIZ = Animal Powers, Shapeshifting and Swan Maidens

The Norns deliver or fulfil Fate, but do they create it? Is there a power greater even than the Norns or do the Norns work with the very fabric of the Universe, following impersonal cosmic laws? Here we find animal powers and allies and shapeshifting, in the terminology of the Old Norse traditions: the *fylfja, kinfylgja* and *hugr*

REID – SOL = Solar Cycles and Solar Flares
The Chariot of the Sun

The concept of both Sunna (the sun) and Máni (the moon) riding in celestial chariots is an ancient and appears frequently in petroglyphs and other Scandinavian artifacts from the Bronze Age. The *Trundholm sun chariot* is the most famous example. Solar cycles are nearly periodic 11-year changes in the Sun's activity, based on the number of sunspots present on the Sun's surface. Solar flares are large explosions from the surface of the sun that emit intense bursts of electromagnetic radiation.[37]

REID – TYR = Arrow of Time and Time Travel
Tyr's Mission and Viking Raids

The theoretical physicist Sean Carroll says that the Arrow of Time has the same origin as the Arrow of Space. We use the word "time" frequently in everyday language but the real puzzles arise when we consider the *properties of time,* such as pas/present/future. We can affect the future but not the past. Carroll lectures on the possibility of time travel and the concept of the multiverse.[38] The wheels of justice grind slowly. The Vikings gave English the word "raid", which is still in use today and etymologically related to REID.

REID – BJARKA = Rites of Passage for Women and Girls

In the Slavic tradition the birch tree plays a central role. Every part has healing properties. Ailing people were beaten with birch branches *(Finnish people still "whisk" themselves in the sauna!)* Infusions and concoctions were made to cure illnesses. People drank birch juice. Birch was also used in folk magic as a love potion. Birch was also used in funerals: a coffin was often laid out with birch leaves and brooms. The pillow placed under the head of the deceased person was stuffed with birch leaves. Sometimes a birch tree was even planted on a grave.[39]

REID – EH = Sleipnir Moving Between the Worlds
Corpse Roads

Sleipnir is Odin's eight-legged horse. He is described as *the best of horses*. In *Sigrdrífumál*, the Valkyrie Sigrdrífa tells the hero Sigurðr that runes should be cut "on Sleipnir's teeth and on the sledge's strap-bands.[40] A corpse road is a footpath, connecting parishioners in outlying locations to churches, followed by pallbearers when they carried a coffin to church. It was believed that any field used as a coffin road would fail to produce good corps. Those paths were also associated with spirits, wraiths and ghost stories.[41]

REID – MADR = Karma, Lineages and Kinship
Ancestral Pathways and Pilgrimage

This is the axis of lifetimes, life cycles and even much longer cycles (eras, epochs, eons); also of kinship, clans and lineages and ancestral imprints running through many generations.

The jury is still out on reincarnation in the Old Norse Traditions. Some scholars claim they did not have the concept at all, but we do have saga cycles where the protagonists reincarnate and the story continues. Shamanic healing work has taught me that in each lifetime the soul works on several karmic themes simultaneously and those themes can be formulated as runic axes.

REID – LAGU = Travelling by Water
Boats, Ships, Water Sports

(Ancestral) Memory
The Moon as Measurer of Time
Here we experience the different properties (and manifestations) of waves, including waves in physics, mathematics and society. Our sense of self and continuity only exists courtesy of time and memory.

REID – ING = The Wagon Procession of Nerthus (Fertility Rite)
The Unconscious and the Collective Unconscious

> *On an island of the sea stands an inviolate grove, in which, veiled with a cloth, is a chariot that none but the priest may touch. The priest can feel the presence of the goddess in this holy of holies, and attends her with the deepest reverence as her chariot is drawn along by cows. Then follow days of rejoicing and merrymaking in every place that she condescends to visit and sojourn in. No one goes to war, no one takes up arms; every iron object is locked away. Then, and then only, are peace and quiet known and welcomed, until the goddess, when she has had enough of the society of men, is restored to her sacred precinct by the priest. After that, the chariot, the vestments, and (believe it if you will) the goddess herself, are cleansed in a secluded lake. This service is performed by slaves who are immediately afterwards drowned in the lake. Thus, mystery begets terror and a pious reluctance to ask what that sight.* [42]

Freud saw, what he called, *The Unconscious* as a primary source of human behaviour. Think of our conscious mind as the tip of an iceberg, the rest is there but floats below the surface in murky icy deep waters. Carl Jung coined the term *The Collective Unconscious*. He saw this as a vast collection of knowledge and imagery that every person is born with and is shared by all human beings due to ancestral experience.

REID – ODAL= Finding the Balance Between Home and Away
Property Maintenance

Some people are natural born travellers and others are home bodies. Here we navigate a balance between comfort and new experiences, between continuity and starting over. In terms of relationships this axis refers to choices: *am I staying or leaving? Or could we go travelling together and heal, change or rejuvenate our relationship?*

REID – DAGAZ = The Journey to Enlightenment
Axial Precession

For many people spiritual practices enhance both their life quality and ability to cope with adversity. Other people call spirituality woo woo, fantasy or opium for the masses.

REID – FE = Cattle Herders
Flexibility of Location
People Driven from their Lands

This axis describes the shift from the nomadic lifestyle of hunter-gatherers to farming and settled life (in the Mesolithic and Neolithic period). This was a gradual development stretching over thousands of years. During the Covid-19 Pandemic people were encouraged to work from home and this brought about a reappraisal of location and work-life balance. Another big current theme is decolonization (of places and the Western mind).

KEN

Pine torch, blacksmith, forge, creativity.

KEN – GIFU = The Gift of Metallurgy
The Blacksmith and the Beauty

Metallurgy is the branch of science and technology concerned with the properties of metals and their production and purification. Hephaestus is probably the best-known blacksmith god. Like the dwarfs in Norse cosmology, he creates power objects for the gods. He built his forge in a volcano and caused volcanic eruptions. He was lame and considered "ugly" but marries Aphrodite, the beautiful goddess of love.

KEN – WYNJA = Tools for a Well-Run Farm

This axis celebrates creativity. We treasure objects crafted by fire from metal (horse shoes, jewellery etc.) The Vikings had elaborate ornamented shields. Charms date back to the Neolithic era, when hunters carried interesting objects for good luck.[43]

KEN – GIFU

Here we encounter the dwarfs *(dvergar)*, who forge amazing tools for the gods but they are known to request payment in the form of sleeping with a goddess. In Norse cosmology every gift requires a return gift.

KEN – HAGAL = The Forge of Initiation

This zone is a place of danger and great transformation.

Some Serbian witches call in the Devil when someone is in danger or serious trouble. According to the local belief system, only the Devil has the power to stop evil, death and illness because he is a master of evil (and of all things bad in the material world). He commands the powers of magic and can assist 'his people'. Many consider this to be a very dangerous option, and they do it only if they have no other choice.[44]

KEN – NAUD = The Necessity of Initiation

Human beings need baptisms of fire. Initiations are portals to the next stage of life. Initiations drive and accelerate the evolutions of human consciousness.

KEN – IS = Cold Fire, Ice Burn and Frost Bite

Blacksmiths use both water (LAGU) and oil for quenching hot metal. Sometimes they use salt-baths (HAGAL – LAGU) as well. Spiritual teacher Joseph Rael said that cold truth is the winter season of the North.[45]

Touching something extremely cold (e.g. metal), can damage our skin and cause ice burn.

KEN – JARA = Meteorites and Blood
Iron as The Enemy of Fairy

Anyone who has seen the 2014 movie Maleficent will know that iron burns fairies and iron chains can hold a dragon captive.[46] In some parts of Britain, the introduction of iron tools was resisted for centuries, as farmers believed that the "evil" they contained would poison the soil. By mass iron is the most common element on earth and it forms much of Earth's outer and inner core. An iron needle floating in a bowl of water can act as a compass and iron turns our blood red. (KEN – LAGU)

KEN – PERTRHA = Brisingamen
The Blacksmith and Forge Inside the Mountain
Rock, (Precious) Stones, Minerals and Mining
The Trickster or Rebel God Chained to the Mountain

The dwarfs are described as dark in appearance. They live underground in Svartalfheim, (a labyrinthine complex of mines and forges). Four dwarves (Dvalinn, Alfrik, Berlingr, and Grer) forged the famous necklace *Brísingamen* (brísingr is a poetic term for fire or amber) for Freyj. In return (GIFU) she spent one night with every single one of them.

KEN – EOH = The Pine Torch and Yew Needles

The tools and weapons crafted by Iron Age smiths were more primitive than its 21st century counterparts but the core technique of metalworking remain the same. Yew is an evergreen tree and parts of it (bark, branch, tips and needles) are used to make medicine. Taxol (a prescription drug for treating ovarian and breast cancer) is made from yew. Yew is also used to promote menstruation, cause abortion and treat parasitic infections (despite safety concerns).

KEN – ALGIZ = The Wild Protector of Blacksmiths

To paraphrase a Siberian proverb: the Blacksmith is the older brother of the shaman, they are from the same nest. The Slavic god Veles becomes identified with the Devil after Christianisation. He invented and governed the art of blacksmithing. (Therefore, there is a persistent belief that "the Devil invented blacksmithing".) Veles is depicted wearing a black cape reaching all the way to the ground. Ethnologists explain that this cape is really a rope in which the dead are coiled. Like Hephaistos he is lame. In the Gnostic worldview, lameness became a symbol of the demiurge, who *hammers the material world into existence.* The word demiurge comes from Greek (δημιουργός) and means artisan or craftsman.

KEN – SOL = The Divine Spark in all of Creation

Saulė is a powerful Slavic deity. As the sun goddess she is responsible for all life on Earth. She is the patroness of unfortunate souls, especially orphans. The Lithuanian and Latvian words for "the world", (*pasaulis* and *pasaule*), are translated as "[a place] under the Sun".[47]

KEN – TYR = The Tools & Weapons of the Spiritual Warrior Disability and Super Powers

How we define *weapons of spiritual warfare* depends on your belief system and how you perceive your adversary. is your enemy some person or force outside you or is it something inside you: ignorance, self-obsession, failure to reflect and engage in shadow work? You are the blacksmith of your own spiritual armoury or toolkit. In Norse cosmology there is a close connection between loss of a body part and the acquisition of supernatural powers. I once taught a webinar series exploring this phenomenon.

KEN – BJARKA = The Seed of Duality Planted in Both Maiden and Cosmic Womb
The Female Blacksmith
Scorch Marks

The Christian dogma of the pure Virgin Mother and the Immaculate Conception is somewhat odd. It refers to "unsoiled goods", yet these "goods" concerned must be penetrated/soiled/ transformed if Life (humanity) is to continue. KEN is written with two strokes and "half of Rune ING". The Seed of Duality points to a crossroads in an energetic field of potentiality. It also highlights the female aspect of the blacksmith, a female consort or female blacksmith.

KEN – EH = The Farrier
Horse Shoe

A *horse blacksmith* is a *farrier* who has the specialist skills to shape metal shoes for hooves.

KEN – MADR = An Eruption or Breakthrough in Consciousness
Mass-Production

Something that erupts from within seeks healing. This is what disease really is. In ancestral healing work we find trauma, disturbances and negative imprints. (KEN: scorch marks). Those issues are on repeat. They make life far more difficult than it needs to be.

KEN – LAGU = Human Blood & Haemoglobin
The Tricky Marriage of Fire and Water
Unrequited Passion

The marriage of Fire and Water is tricky. We see this concept play out in astrology when fire signs date water signs. Things can get steamy or end prematurely. When the relationship goes right, water signs can help fire signs to express their emotions and follow their intuition. In return fire signs can spark water signs into activity. Water can be used to extinguish fires but fire can dry up water so it evaporates.

KEN – ING = The Forceps and Bellows
The Erupting and Fertilising Principle
Rune ING looks like a diamond. Bisect it with a horizontal line and you have KEN: "both a grave mound and the mound of Venus", passion and destruction. Sometimes a new paradigm requires a forceps delivery.

KEN – ODAL = The Axis of Iðavöllr
Artisans Crafting Domestic Objects
The Forge as Temple
The *Völuspá* describes *Iðavöllr* (Splendour-plain) as the meeting-place of the Æsir, where they built shrines and temples, as well as forges to make iron tools. The surviving gods will meet here after the cataclysmic events of Ragnarök and build the shining hall of Gimle. In Serbia and the Balkan region, the ritual knife is one of the most important ritual tools in folk magic and witchcraft. Witches wore those ceremonial knives, blade pointing upwards, during their nocturnal flights (for protection). Witches will move those knives over sick people, to chase away illness, for astral surgery and other types of magical healing.[48]

KEN – DAGAZ = Enlightened Creativity
The Divine Creative Force
Alchemy and Transmutation

> *"The creative process shrivels in the absence of continual dialogue with the soul. And creativity is what makes life worth living".* -Marion Woodman[49]

Ordeals faced at KEN pose an ego-death. To create from an egoic state means creating from a place of confined consciousness. Co-creating with spirit brings better outcomes.

KEN – FE = Cattle Owner Turns Investment Banker
Cattle owners are no longer the wealthiest people. This privilege falls to billionaires, media moguls, rock stars, neurosurgeons and investment bankers. We have a Rich List. Many people do manual work to support their families. Not every working person has a "career".

GIFU

Gift, exchange, sacred reciprocity, hieros gamos, crossroads.

GIFU – WYNJA = The Joys and Fruits of a Happy Marriage
Freyja, Frigg and Gefjon
The sacred marriage between King and Goddess of the Land occurs here, planting the seeds of peace and plenty.[50] The (Christian) Pax Christi symbol can be viewed as a bind rune consisting of GIFU and WYNJA.

GIFU – HAGAL = Where Catastrophes Seed Renewal
The Generosity of the Witch
Gifu is the rune of gifts, exchange and interaction. This axis also has an erotic dimension which replicates the sacred marriage between a god and goddess in marriages on earth. Rune HAGAL refers to another type of encounter. A "cosmic hail storm" upends our life. The resulting losses make space for new beginnings (and new connections).

GIFU – NAUD = Synchronicity and Serendipity
Happy Accidents

Jung defined *synchronicity* as an "acausal connecting (togetherness) principle", a "meaningful coincidence of two or more events where something other than the probability of chance is involved."[51] *Serendipity* relies on the intersection between wisdom and chance to accidentally find something of interest or value. There are two variations:

1. Looking for something and finding it in an unexpected way
2. Looking for something and finding something entirely different but very useful.[52]

GIFU – IS = Surgical Scissors made of Ice

I perceive this as rune GIFU turning into ice and then opening and closing, like a sharp pair of surgical scissors. This is a precision instrument. It cuts what no longer serves. It also cuts any unhealthy cords which connect people and keep them stuck. Healers can use these scissors as a sacred tool (gift from Skaði).

GIFU – JARA = Sif's Hair
The Gift of Grain
Giving Back to Plants and Trees

Sif (Thor's wife) probably represents the fields of golden wheat, cut down by the scythe during the harvest. A gardener reminded me recently that if we grow too many seedlings, we use scissors to cut snip some, so others have space to grow.

> *"Scatter the grain, I say, while I sing;* [JARA – ASS]
> *The bones of Delphi I am scattering"* [PERTHRA – ASS] //
> *This brazen wheel I whirl, so as before* [REID]
> *Restless may he be, whirled about my door* [REID][53]

GIFU – PERTRHA = The Gift of Cave Time

The early people of the Low Countries thought of dead people as literally being planted in the Earth as seeds (during funerals). On this axis we step away from the busyness and demands of the world. We allow ourselves *cave time,* the opportunity to retrieve (or connect with) the more dormant or hidden parts of ourselves. There is no Bear Rune but on this axis I dream in the embrace of Bears and the Mountain Mother. On this axis we can sometimes revive or reverse things that appear to be dead. Animals thought to be extinct but then found alive and thriving occasionally make the headlines.[54]

GIFU – EOH = Gifts of Trees

Trees provide oxygen and forests help remove fossil fuel emissions and other pollutants. One large tree can provide a day's supply of oxygen for up to four people. Trees provide wood for carpentry and provide shelter for many creatures. Even fallen trees become insect hotels and hosts for fungi.[55]

GIFU – ALGIZ = Axis of the Blót
The Gifts of Antlered Beings and Wild Gods
Spoils of the Hunt
Animal sacrifice

Deer gift us meat, fur and antlers for carving. Working with the Reindeer Mother was a life-changing gift for me.[56] The Old Norse people sacrificed animals during their blóts (offering ceremonies) and blood was sprinkled all over the place and those present, as a live-giving blessing. A *blót* could be dedicated to specific gods, ancestors or the *landvaettir* (spirits of the land).[57]

GIFU – SOL = The Gifts from the Sun

Sunlight is a necessity for life on Earth. The immense mass of the Sun keeps all other planets in orbit. If she disappeared, the Earth (and all other planets) would retain their forward motion and shoot into outer space in a straight line. Earth would enter a never-ending *Fimbulvetr* ("mighty winter"), a signal that Ragnarok is imminent. Oceans would freeze over and Earth would have an average global temperature of -400º F or -240 °Celsius. And did I mention harsh cosmic radiation?

GIFU – TYR = The Gifts of the Spiritual Warrior
The Sacred Marriage of an Ancient Goddess and Newcomer Warrior-God

Tyr sacrificed an arm to the wolf and delayed Ragnarok. He made his sacrifice in the literal meaning of the word, "making sacred". The Norse had a custom of carving the TYR rune into weapons for protection and divine support. The sign of the cross was made over newborn children and at weddings and funerals, as a blessing.[58]

GIFU – BJARKA = The Gifts of the Birch Tree

Birch branches are pleated together and used in matchmaking and courting rituals.

In Scandinavia people used to make many beautiful items from *björknäver* (the outer bark of birch trees, the genus Betula): storage boxes, bags, canoes, writing materials and even building materials. The bark is both strong and water-resistant. It also contains substances used for medicinal or chemical purposes. Bark containers have fungicidal properties which help preserve any food placed inside.[59] The leaves of the silver birch tree can be infused to make a tea that treats infection and stimulates a healthy vitality. Early peoples stitched the bark together to make food vessels and canoes for hunting. In spring, the sap was made into mead, and the fresh cambial tissue became bread.

GIFU – EH = The Kiss of Death"

Gifts for Dead People and from Dead People

The Balkan states have a strong tradition of offering gifts to dead people. There is a rock gate in Serbia, which acts as public portal to the underworld. Local people perform an ancient ritual there, to send gifts to the dead.[60] On this axis we also find the "poison gift" of (deadly) sexually transmitted diseases. Last but not least there is *corrupt sacrifice.* This refers to a miasma (spiritual stain or contagion) created by the collective fury of the wrongfully dead.[61]

GIFU – MADR = The Gifts (and burdens) of Our Ancestors

In an ideal world, we make offerings to our ancestors in return for the gifts they gave us (such as life!) and we practice ancestral healing work. Some indigenous peoples speak of our ancestors living in our blood. Their experiences pool in our ancestral field and colour our experiences on Earth.

GIFU – LAGU = The Gift of Water

Water was present long before human beings existed. All life is said to have originated in the primordial waters or "soup".

GIFU – ING = Sacrifices to Norse God Freyr

Freyr received sacrifices and offerings on specific occasions during the year. During harvest festivals a boar was sacrificed to Freyr, his sacred animal.

GIFU – ODAL = The Construction Sacrifice

In Latvia building a church required a human sacrifice. Boys and girls were asked "if they wanted to look after the keys of the Church". If a child said yes, (s)he was walled up in a pillar. There was a saying that "Every church requires a sacrifice" and it was assumed that the victim transformed into a supernatural guardian spirit of the building (the ODAL – ASS Axis).[62]

GIFU – DAGAZ = The Gift of Enlightenment

All spiritual paths promise the gift of (a degree of) enlightenment if one meets the challenges of this lifetime (and possibly other lifetimes on Earth). Where the runes meet modern spirituality, one could say that this axis might promise that your fate was carved for your greater good, not "by harsh Norns". This axis then acts as a counterpart to Ørlǫg. It offers the promise that we can transcend what "has been carved".

GIFU – FE = Axis of the Blót

We need to give, if we hope to receive. That is the underlying (transactional) concept of a *blót*. By offering to the Norse gods, we hope to secure a good harvest, fertility and healthy cattle. A *blót* typically involved the ritual slaughter of an animal followed by the cooking and eating of the meat. Divination was performed during *blóts* and the gods were consulted on important matters.

WYNJA

Joy, harmony, contentment, inner and outer peace, Frigg's Rune.

WYNJA – HAGAL = Finding Joy in Endings and Rebirth Valuing the Regeneration Brought by Destruction

Here we hear the cackle of the Village Witch! Most people dread destruction and try to avoid it. This keeps people stuck in unhappy marriages or jobs that drain them of life force. Cosmic destruction in occurs if we get too comfortable (individually or collectively) or too stuck. Many people would not live their true purpose, had destruction (a crisis, divorce or serious illness) not forced them to change direction.

WYNJA – NAUD = Where Joy Touches Necessity

Joy and Necessity generally feel like opposites, but Khalil Gibran said:

> *"You pray in your distress and in your need; would that you might also pray in the fullness of your joy and in your days of abundance."*[63]

WYNJA – IS = Solidified Joy

This axis holds the memories of all the occasions where we experienced joy or bliss. Those nuggets of luminosity and brighten difficult days. People can get frozen in trauma, but the opposite can occur too. People become so attached to the good memories that they are in denial about a relationship no longer working.[64]

WYNJA – JARA

We experience the delight of reaping what we have sown (assuming we have sown the right seeds and watered them tenderly and consistently).

WYNJA – PERTRHA = The Joys of Cave Time

This axis is the "bear cave" we retreat to when we need to recharge or replenish ourselves and touch our core, our inner mountain.

WYNJA – EOH = The Joy of Trees

This axis expresses the joy of forests and all "God's creatures, great and small".

WYNJA – ALGIZ = The Joys of the Wild and of Rewilding

"This is where the wild things are", to quote Maurice Sendak. "Re-wilding" has become a buzz word: we now actively work on rewilding nature, ourselves, our relationship to religion etc. A related word, used in a similar context, is re-enchanting. People speak about the need for reenchanting nature. I don't agree. The enchantment *is always present,* but we humans have been conditioned to close our eyes to it. It is a power greater than humans.

> *In times of joy, all of us wished we possessed a tail we could wag.*
>
> *-W. H. Auden*[65]

WYNJA – SOL = Eternity's Sunrise

This axis expresses delight, awe and gratitude at Sunna rising every day.

> *He who binds to himself a joy Does the winged life destroy;*
> *But he who kisses the joy as it flies Lives in eternity's sun rise.*
>
> *-William Blake*[66]

WYNJA – TYR = The Joy and Fulfilment of Right Action

Tyr embodies the principle of right action.

WYNJA – BJARKA = Joyful Parenting and Domestic Harmony

This is the energy signature of the Cosmic Mother: domestic harmony and a secure, loving space for children to grow up.

WYNJA – EH = A Good Death

This is the axis of death doulas and high quality (compassionate and inspired) end-of-life care. We need to shake off our death-denial and think seriously about the way we want to die.[67]

WYNJA – MADR

My own life has taught me that joy is an intentional act, closely linked to appreciation and gratitude. I make a point of seeing the joy and beauty in small things, of not taking my blessings for granted. I do this on dark and difficult days too. That is the core teaching of this axis.

WYNJA – LAGU = Where Joy and Grief Walk Hand in Hand
This is *the Joy-Grief Axis.*

> *"Grief is subversive, undermining the quiet agreement to behave and be in control of our emotions. It is an act of protest that declares our refusal to live numb and small. There is something feral about grief, something essentially outside the ordained and sanctioned behaviours of our culture. Because of that, grief is necessary to the vitality of the soul. Contrary to our fears, grief is suffused with life-force.... It is not a state of deadness or emotional flatness. Grief is alive, wild, untamed and cannot be domesticated. It resists the demands to remain passive and still. We move in jangled, unsettled, and riotous ways when grief takes hold of us. It is truly an emotion that rises from the soul."*
>
> -Francis Weller[68]

WYNJA – ING = The Fulltrui
ING is Freyr's rune. He does not only rule the grains of the earth, but he also brings sunshine and peace among men. This is the axis of *Fulltrui*, a word often translated as patron deity. The word means "fully trusted one" (in contemporary Icelandic it means representative). A human being enters a committed and inclusive (meaning one focusses on this one deity to the exclusion of other gods) relationship with a deity, but please note that this relationship is always chosen by the deity, not the human being. It is a soul contract which may well extend into the Afterlife, and this should never be undertaken lightly.[69]

WYNJA – ODAL = The Joys Of Belonging
Oh, the joy of knowing where our home is and where we belong. Robert Frost said it perfectly: "Home is the place where, when you have to go there, they have to take you in."

WYNJA – DAGAZ = Equilibrium & the Elegance of Balance
This axis is the point of balance. Swedish has a word for this: *lagom*. It means just right, "enough" in the sense of something being perfectly balanced or a task perfectly met.

WYNJA – FE = Axis of Abundance and the Good Times
The joy we experience at times of abundance: when life treats us kindly and we are well-provided for, well-resourced enough to live our dreams.

HAGAL

Literally hail, sudden cataclysmic change, rune of the Pregnant Hag.

HAGAL – IS
The Rainbow Bridge Is An Ice Bridge At Night
The Winter Witch
Heimdallr Guards Bifrost (A Rainbow By Day And A Trembling Ice Bridge At Night). The *rainbow bridge* is the (slanted) crossbar of Rune HAGAL: a bridge between opposites, order and chaos, construction and destruction, forever tilting and shifting.

HAGAL – JARA = The Pregnant Hag Bears Seasonal Fruits
HAGAL is The Pregnant Hag, cycling through all stages of development in a calendar year. She brings fruit and tough love, accompanied by Old European goddesses such as Norse Hel and the Germanic Frau Holle.

HAGAL – PERTRHA = The Millstone as a Cult Object
Koschei the Deathless Riding His Horse in the Mountains
Pairs of deities were once perceived as dividing the year between them. Baba Yaga has a consort: "Koshchei the Deathless": ugly,

bony, immortal, and evil. His soul had been hidden on an island far away. Koschei appears as immortal and undefeatable (unless a human hero locates his hidden soul).[70]

HAGAL – EOH = The Witch Tree & the Forest Witch

The brittle bones of the Elder Witch were known to house spirits, in particular near the joints of the branches. One German name for it was "Elves Grave".[71] Sambucus Nigra is the Black Elder Tree and is a veritable apothecary. Polish ancestors gave their sorrows and sins to the elder tree.[72]

HAGAL – MADR = The Witch as Scapegoat

Witches, healers, midwives and herbalists have always been perceived as possessing superpowers. They were blamed (and punished) for things going wrong in the village.

HAGAL – EH = Protecting the Dead from Witches

A cross was made from elder wood and held or carried before the coffin in funeral processions. It was sometimes buried with a child, to protect it from the attention of malevolent witches (accused of digging up small corpses to harvest fat for flying ointment).

HAGAL – ALGIZ = The Divine Hag Milking Her Herd of Deer[73]

Animal Materia Magica

Witches magically use body parts of animals. In Serbia attention is paid to the way the animal died: if it died a natural death, it is used for positive purposes because it didn't lose its magical power and it didn't suffer while dying. If wolves tore a ram apart, its horns will be used for negative purposes like "wars between witches". Animal claws and teeth are used to make protective amulets.[74]

HAGAL – SOL = Axis of a Solar Eclipse

A solar eclipse made people fear that a wolf had devoured Sunna. We face our worst fears but, miraculously, the Sun returns and brings hope.

HAGAL – TYR = Battles Between Witches

This axis describes power struggles for dominance between witches for the following reasons: conflicts due to clients, attacks to re-establish a damaged reputation for power, spells to address village gossip and magical work to influence unsolved court cases. People often consult a witch when they feel magically attacked. The most surprising thing about *malefic magic* is that the powers invoked, and the being contacted are the same as for healing: The Forest Mother, Water Mother, Great Water Spirit, Fairies etc. These entities are neutral by nature and will grant the request of the witch. The witch only (and always) seeks to restore balance in her life (or community).[75]

HAGAL – BJARKA = The Hedge Mother
An Illness or Disease Being the Healer

We meet Freyja (the First Witch), Mother Holle and Perchta. Germanic people used the term "hedge riding" for witches travelling to other worlds. UR is the Cosmic Witch Mother who creates the Universe. HAGAL is the Witch Mother who directs, intervenes and changes the course of human lives (and civilizations) by means of ordeals.

HAGAL – EH = Baba Yaga & Norse Elli
Death And Arousal

This is the Hag in her death-bringing manifestation. In the poem *Gylfaginning* (*Prose Edda*), Snorri Sturluson describes a meeting between Utgarda-Loki and old giantess called Elli. One day Thor is challenged to wrestle Elli. The frail-looking old woman defeats him. Utgarda-Loki ends the match: it is futile to fight old age![76]

HAGAL – MADR = Our Witch Ancestors
Outsiders and Stepping Outside Societal Expectations
Witchcraft

This axis circumscribes all human beings who are witches, healers, herbalists, midwives, shamans etc. The medical profession, as we know it today, is young. Folk healers once took care of medical needs. HAGAL is also a gateway for people who are ostracised or step outside norms to become recluses and tricksters. Criminals also play the role of Trickster.

HAGAL – LAGU = Witch Blood and Witch Lineages

Knowledge of witchcraft is passed on between generations in families, where some people are known to have 'witch blood'.[77]

HAGAL – ING = The Pregnant Hag and Witch's Drum

This is the cosmic Seed of the Universe. In Norse mythology nine universes were "seeded" and destroyed (before the current one). In her womb the Pregnant Hag carries the unborn child but also the Seed of Death. (By conceiving new life, we also create a future death).

HAGAL – ODAL

Rune ODAL refers to an enclosed private or domestic space, a secure home. The word *hag* is etymologically related to an enclosure, hedge or boundary as well (think of *hedge riding*). Apotropaic marks (of protection) were scratched on doors and buildings to keep witches away.

HAGAL – DAGAZ = The Dark Hag as the Mother of the Bright Day

Here we find the Divine Mother and her Son: Night (Nott) gives birth to Day (Dagr), in a cosmic dance between sacred feminine and sacred masculine

HAGAL – FE = Paying the Witch's Fee

"Wealth is desirable but disruptive, it is the fire of the sea and the path of the serpent". *Icelandic Rune Poem*[78] Witches work closely with the principle of give-and-take in the Universe (their services are not free).

NAUD

**Need, necessity, the rune of the Norns.
Restriction. Tightening the belt. Hardship and lack or resources or options. Feeling thwarted, unable to follow our desire or plan.**

NAUD – IS = A Master Class in Self-Awareness

This axis imposes restriction and a freezing of something (resources or personal needs). Shift our focus from ego to being of service. In certain situations, I view Rune IS as the solidified self, the "I" that speaks in the first pronoun.

NAUD – JARA = Great Necessity and Food Insecurity

The Inuit peoples had a word which translates as The Great Necessity: it refers to the need for other life forms to die so I can eat and live. Going vegan does not change that: many plants die, for someone to eat a plant-based diet for life. Many people in our high-tech world still face food insecurity.

NAUD – PERTHRA = Ancestral Wisdom Carved in Stone

Our ancestors carved images in rock (or stone). Sweden has an abundance of petroglyphs. Siberia has mysterious deer stones as well. In the Baltic countries large stones were often carved with symbols of suns and snakes.[79]

NAUD – EOH = The Mead Tree and the "Niu Ividi"
Maria Kvilhaug translates this phrase, "niu iviði", from the Vǫluspá, as *Nine Witches Within Wood.* The Vǫlva speaking here is older than the present universe, referred to as the Mead Tree or Yggdrasil, the physical manifestation of our universe symbolized by a tree. Before our current universe, there were nine previous worlds (heimir), and those worlds were identifiable by nine "iviði".[80]

NAUD – ALGIZ = The Norns and the Valkyries
Valkyrja means "chooser of the slain". The Valkyries assist Freyja by flying over the battlefields and deciding who will die on a given day. Rune ALGIZ is usually linked to the elk or moose but its shape of the rune also resembles a crow's foot or a swan in flight and hints at swan maidens, Valkyries and other "bird women".

NAUD – SOL = The Sun Sustaining Life on Earth
The sun is necessity, not a luxury. Without her light and heat, our beautiful planet would be as barren as Mars or Mercury.

NAUD – TYR = Carving Battle Fate
Military Discipline
Duty and Honour
Here the fate of warriors is carved. Who are the warriors in Western culture? Who embodies the Viking values of duty and honour? This is also the axis of military service and protecting our community and country.

NAUD – BJARKA = The Sorrowful Mother
On this axis of the Pietà we find mothers raising their children under harrowing circumstances (armed conflict, famine, lack of clean drinking water etc.) Seeing your child suffer brings unique forms of grief.

NAUD – EH = Death as "The Great Necessity"
Ontological dilemma: without death an ever-aging population would walk the earth (or would everyone eventually be in wheelchairs?) And what if there are no younger people to provide all the old age or dementia care needed?)

NAUD – MADR = The Axis of Ancestral Trickster Figures
Loki acts in service to the Norns. I meet him at Rune NAUD. Tricksters act as the fertilising power (of chaos), in service to Necessity.

NAUD – LAGU = Erosion as a Trickster
The actions of Loki can be viewed as (cultural) erosion: he strips off layers and exposes, he shifts and steals. He brings both treasures and disasters. This axis brings a stripping and shedding of skins. We can no longer hide or pretend to be something/someone we are not. Discomfort is a powerful teacher.

NAUD – ING = The Seeds of Necessity and Fated Events
On this axis we find all seeds: of change, new life and death, disaster and abundance etc. Also, all technology for assisted fertility.

NAUD – ODAL = The Axis of Hubris
Here human beings pit themselves against fated limits. Modern science and technology play a huge role in this: weapons of mass destruction, AI, cloning, genetically modified foods etc.

NAUD – DAGAZ = The Need for True Enlightenment
Perhaps true enlightenment lies in a moral compass and strong sense of community and kinship. Limits and boundaries exist to keep us all safe. Not every limit is an invitation for someone to break it.

NAUD – FE = The Norn Called Skuld
Wergild (Reparation, Compensation)

The name of the Norn called Skuld means *debt* (not future). Paying our (financial and spiritual) debts creates a (far) better future for all. Also, downsizing to change our work-life balance.

IS
Ice.

IS – PERTHRA = Hibernation

In Norse mythology and folklore many supernatural (otherworld) beings live under rocks, in caves and in crevasses and crevices. This is a powerful liminal zone. Grizzly bears hibernate in a cave, crevice, hollow tree or under the root mass of a tree) and polar bears hibernate in dens dug out of deep snow.

IS – EOH = The Tundra, Taiga & Permafrost
Hypothermia
A Polar Desert

In the subarctic zone we find evergreens: conifers, pine, spruce, junipers. This is the axis of the treeline and permafrost, places without trees. Here polar explorers risk their lives to gain unique experiences of survival.

IS – ALGIZ = The (Extinct) Animals of the Ice Age
Animals at Risk of Extinction

This axis asks us: what is the human factor in animal extinction? Did we cause extinction, or did we hasten the inevitable?

IS – SOL = Where Ice meets Fire

In Norse mythology the world was created from the meeting of Fire and Ice. Here we experience sudden the flashes of insight that strike us like lightning (lightbulb moments).

IS – TYR = Frozen or Stuck in the Spiritual Warrior Archetype

Some people embrace the key concepts of a spiritual path but do not allow a natural unfolding, a flow with change. Being a warrior or activist can become a cherished identity people are not willing to release, long after the desired change has occurred.

IS – BJARKA = The Ice Queen or Icicle Woman

A Frigid Marriage

This is the axis of a cold woman with a heart made of ice, whose weapons area sharp tongue and icicle. She makes an excellent sniper or forensic pathologist. Her unique form of healing consists of sharp-shooting and dissecting. She is a truth-seeker but provides no comfort to those who crave her truth.

IS – EH = Death by Hypothermia (Literal or Symbolic)

Literally speaking this axis refers to death by hypothermia. On a more symbolic level this refers to exploring any frozen wastelands in our psyche. Sleipnir, Odin's eight-legged horse, can also help us explore *inner* worlds.

IS – MADR = Inner and Outer Self

The Detached Observer

Here we find the detached observer and people perceived as "cold" (unsympathetic and heartless). These people might be emotionally frozen after traumatic experiences that were beyond their ability to process.

IS – LAGU = Skadi and Njord

Supercooled Water

The Secret Life of Ice

One day Skaði arrives at Asgard to seek restitution for the killing of her father, Thiazi. She could have any god she desired (as her husband), but must choose him only by his feet. She picks Njord, a god of the sea. Their marriage is short-lived.

IS – ING = Seed Dormancy

Seeds are a storehouse of potential. They can slumber for long periods in the earth, in ice, or even in storage jars (seed dormancy).

IS – ODAL = A Home in the Arctic or an Emotionally Cold Home

Here people had a home where they did not receive adequate emotional nourishment. They often grow up feeling like outsiders.

IS – DAGAZ = Ice as a Precision Tool on the Road to Enlightenment

I see a scalpel made of ice (a very sharp icicle) that cuts away the webs of illusion – including all the veils of delf-deception. This process is very painful, but ultimately liberating. Were ice and water the first mirrors for Stone Age people?

IS – FE = The Cost of Individuality

This axis signals to *lean years,* where we do not prosper, despite planting the right seeds. Also, the cost of expressing our authentic selves in a complex or hostile world.

JARA

Harvest, year.

JARA – PERTRHA = The Fruits of the Mountain Mothers

Jara means harvest and it etymologically related to the Old Norse word for year: ár. Mother Earth sustains all life forms. Up to the eighteenth century, Lithuanians offered gifts to Žemyna upon the birth of a child. The Earth was kissed in the morning and evening.[81]

JARA – EOH = The Axis Mundi or World Axis

Yggdrasil is the *axis mundi* or world axis. EOH is etymologically related to the word yew. Yggdrasil acts a cognitive map offering paths and portals to other worlds. *Climbing this axis, we pick the fruits of our spirit work.*

JARA – ALGIZ = The Harvest Goat

Here we meet Krampus and related (horned, intimidating) figures. Norse people used to slaughter a goat in Yule season but later in history the julbock was made of straw instead. The last sheaf of grain bundled in the harvest was credited with magical properties and saved for the Yule celebrations, called The Yule Goat.

JARA – SOL = No Sunlight, No Harvest

We worry about global warming and climate change. There was a period, called the Late Bronze Age collapse (between 1200-1150 BCE), associated with environmental change, mass migration and the destruction of cities. This sudden change ushered in the Greek Dark Ages, where many states and cultures collapsed.[82]

JARA – TYR = Settlement Challenges

The earlier hunter-gatherer people followed the game and seasons. In the Neolithic period people started living in settlements. They could plant seeds and domesticate animals, but they also faced failed harvests and constantly defending the village from outsiders/invaders/raids.

JARA – BJARKA = The Grain Mother and Provider-Healer Mother of Abundance or Lady Bounty

One manifestation of Mother Earth is the Grain Mother. This axis is the nourishing principle: feeding all mouths and all hungry beings. Food is also our best medicine.

JARA – EH = The Grim Reaper and the Harvest of Souls
Fungi

The Grim Reaper is the "evil twin" of the benevolent soul conductor (psycho pomp), who accompanies the dead to their final destination in the Afterlife. One cuts the down the body, the other "harvests" the soul. This is also the axis of fungi, deeply connected to decay and death.

JARA – MADR = Medicinal Plants
The Mandrake

This is the axis powerful plants (medicinal and poisonous both). The mandrake was said to grow at crossroads where murderers, suicides and witches were buried. It is a transgressive plant. Harvesting the plant incorrectly could cause death and impotence.[83]

JARA – LAGU = Watering Plants
Lunar Phase Gardening

Lunar phase gardening involves following the moon cycles. The waxing moon is for planting seeds which yield fruit overground. The waning moon is for planting root vegetables and for harvesting.

JARA – ING = The Vanir and Fertility Gods

This axis describes the entire cycle from seed to plant to harvest. Germanic folklore tells us that grain crops were under the protection of the Northern nature spirit Hulda (or Bertha). To protect them she would put werewolves on guard, at the boundaries of the fields.[84]

JARA – ODAL = Abundance

If a homestead or farm is well-tended, has the protection of the *Landvaettir* (spirits of the land) and cooperation of the weather spirits, the result is abundance: enough food to feed the settlement and extra food for guests (hospitality was a core virtue in the Viking Age).

JARA – DAGAZ = Where Enlightenment is Harvested

This represents personal growth and true knowledge over "soundbites and Influencers". This axis has a dark twin in DAGAZ – UR, where we move from the broad daylight back into the nourishing darkness of the divine womb.

JARA – FE = (Financial) Security

We are all born into a family system where resources and finances are handled in a particular way. Some families manage this this wisely and others disastrously. Our background provides certain settings that we either internalize, or spend the rest of our life rebelling against. This does not only apply to money, it applies to all the resources we make decisions about (property, time, social connections etc.)

PERTHRA

Rocks, mountains and caves, dice cup, tomb-womb.

PERTHRA – EOH = "Where a Petrified Percht Perches..." Mineralization and Minerals

She (Perchta) perches on oaks and hazel trees...[85] This is also the axis of petrified wood.

PERTHRA – ALGIZ = Petroglyphs and Rock Art

We embark on a tour of antlered beings (and other animals) painted in caves or carved in rock. Check out the Nämforsen site in *Ångermanälven* (Northern Sweden). There are at least 2,595 well-preserved petroglyphs preserved here, believed to be over 6000 years old.[86]

PERTHRA – SOL = Sunlight Turns Trolls into Rocks

In Scandinavian folklore, trolls dwell in remote rocky areas, mountains or caves. They turn to stone when exposed to sunlight, making them creatures of the night and dark places.

PERTHRA – TYR = The Petrified Warrior

In the poem *Hymiskviða,* the Jǫtunn (giant) Hymir is the father of Tyr and the husband of the *gýgr* (giantess) Hróðr. He is the owner of a mile-wide cauldron in which the Æsir wanted to brew beer, so Thor and Týr manage to obtain it.[87]

PERTHRA – BJARKA = Healing Rocks And Stone Goddesses
The Old Norse "Dyngja"

Old Norse farms had a *dyngja* (women's quarters or domestic workroom): dark, often below ground, womb-like spaces where men's fates are shaped by women's work and women's talk.[88]

PERTHRA – EH = Tomb - Womb

Meet the Mother of Cradle and Grave! Also, the axis of the "Hill you are willing to die on".

PERTHRA – MADR = Being Bergtagen
Mountaineers, Rock Climbers, Spelunkers
Herms, Stone Masons, Memorial Stones & Gravestones

Bergtagen (SW) means "spirited away into the mountains". A person gets lost, or inadvertently walks through a portal, and ends up living in a parallel world with mountain spirits or the Fae. There is a dichotomy between the mindset of "conquering a mountain" and truly "entering a mountain": allowing a mountain to communicate with us and become part of our *soulscape.*

PERTHRA – LAGU = The Millstone and Mountain Lakes
Millstones possess unique magical properties. Everything connected to them had magical powers. The water was collected and used in folk medicine or magic. The mud generated was used to treat gynaecological conditions and the mill's Watergate was carried around a village to protect it from storms.[89] Mountains, lakes and the sea (shore) are places where we go to nourish our soul and replenish our inner well. In my rune journal I found a reference to a dream about "a Mud Woman turning to Stone".

PERTHRA – ING = One Axis of the Pregnant Hag
(Her other Axis is Hagal – Ing)
In one sentence: *in the dark cosmic womb the seed of renewal is forever gestating.* The seeds of collective rebirth, (renewal, paradigm shifts), gestate here too

PERTHRA – ODAL = The Womb-Tomb
This populist term is derived from Neolithic burial sites: the chambered burial tomb. Neolithic farmers built burial chambers covered by mounds, suggesting a reverence for birth and the female form.[90]

PERTHRA – DAGAZ = Dark and Bright God Both
"The stone has been rolled back for resurrection". This is the journey from Darkness back into the Light, literally, symbolically and spiritually speaking.

PERTHRA – FE = Faerie Cattle
The Fairy Cattle concept refers to cattle herders being drawn underground. When they reappear, many centuries have passed and everyone they ever knew and loved is gone.[91]

EOH

Yew, axis mundi, spine of the universe.

EOH – ALGIZ = The Horned God of the Forest

The Witch's Protector

"From all old trees proceeds either an owl or the Devil." (Russian proverb)[92] Here be wild gods: the Lord of the Animals, Master of the Game, King of the Beasts etc. Some female versions are: Mistress of the Animals, Lady of the Forest, Animal Keeper etc. In Finland we find "husband-and-wife team" Tapio and Mielikki. Hunters made offerings to these wild gods and made sure not to avoid them by breaking taboos.

Note from my rune journal: *If a tree grew antlers, would we even notice?*

EOH – SOL = The Tree of Longevity Witnesses Every Sunrise on Earth

Most parts of the yew tree are very poisonous. Britain has yew trees that predate the 10th century. Yew trees hollow out as they age but send up basal shoots. Because of their longevity they are associated with everlasting life and vitality. As an "ever-lasting tree of death" they flourish in churchyards.

EOH – TYR = The Eco Warrior

Vårdträd (Swedish for Warden Tree)

Here we find anyone who campaigns on behalf of trees, rainforests and green spaces in cities. This is also the axis of the Warden Tree, *(vårdträd* in Swedish, *tuntre* in Norwegian). Such old trees were believed to protect farms and homesteads from misfortune. Many families in Scandinavia adopted surnames related to trees. My own surname, Almqvist, means *branch of an elm tree.*

EOH – BJARKA = The Forest Mother & Virgin Forests

An old-growth forest is sometimes called a virgin forest. It has attained a great age without significant disturbance and has unique ecological features. We are losing old growth forests (due to logging and greed), which drives many animal species to the brink of extinction.

Note from my rune journal: *Is the axis mundi (world axis) the Forest Maiden's wand of office?*

EOH – EH = Yggdrasil Perceived as Odin's Horse

Dead Wood teems with Life

Odin rides Sleipnir and moves with ease between the Land of the Dead and the Land of the Living. *The claim that over fifty percent of the forest's wood is dead – 'a vast botanical charnel house', to use Schama's phrase – appears somewhat meaningless, as much of what we are talking about is dead and alive at the same time. The dead and the living are constantly in the process of becoming each other.*[93]

EOH – MADR = The Haunter of the Woods

The Green Man and Vegetation Gods

The word *Nemophilist,* or Haunter of the Woods, means someone with a love or fondness for forests. EOH can be viewed as a spinal column and also as the axis on which a human life turns.

EOH – LAGU = Sap Rising

The Forest on the Bottom of the North Sea

By the early Neolithic period, dense forests covered Northern Europe, reaching from the Atlantic Ocean to the Baltic Sea.[94] There is a "forest" on the bottom of the North Sea.[95] According to the beliefs of witches, the Forest Mother is the only force able to stop the Great Water Spirit.[96]

EOH – ING = The Seeds of Pioneer Trees

Birch trees grew from pioneer seeds (carried by the wind, travelling great distances to open spaces after the Ice Age). Behind them came (the seeds of) alder, poplar, willow and Scots pine. Oak came later.[97] Note from my rune journal: *Is Yggdrasil (in some symbolic way) the phallus of Freyr/Ing, the masculine fertilizing principle?*

EOH – ODAL = Wood as Construction Material for Houses

Our ancestors chose their construction material for houses and buildings with immense care. They believed that wood was inhabited by spirits.[98] In Germany it was claimed that three different kinds of wood should be used: stolen wood, purchased wood and wood offered as a gift – otherwise luck would flee (from the house being built IA).[99]

EOH – DAGAZ = Yew as the Tree of Death and Rebirth

As the Tree of Longevity (and world tree) the yew witnesses an (almost) limitless number of sunrises and sunsets.

EOH – FE = The Axis of Thanatos

In Greek mythology Thanatos was the personification of death. In his book "Beyond the Pleasure Principle" in 1920, Freud wrote that human beings had both a life instinct (*eros*) and death instinct (*thanatos*), which compels us to engage in risky and destructive behaviours.[100]

ALGIZ

Protection, animals, moose and antlered creatures, the spirit worker.

ALGIZ – SOL = Beaivi is the Sun Goddess of the Sami People

In Sapmi (the homelands of the Sami people) a white female animal, (usually a reindeer), is sacrificed in honour of

Beaivi, on the day of the winter solstice, to welcome back the sun.

ALGIZ – TYR = The Axis of the Eco Warrior

"I understand the basic function of the hunt: to take someone else's skin that is better than our own and pretend that it is ours. No wonder we made gods of them".[101] On this axis we meet the antlered or horned "eco-warrior priest".

ALGIZ – BJARKA = The Mother of Wild Beasts

Elks are solitary animals. The strongest bond is between mother and calf. Eventually the mother chases the young ones away. In contrast deer are herd animals. They move around in groups.

ALGIZ – EH = Animal Psychopomps

In mythology a psychopomp (soul conductor) is often a god or goddess of the Underworld. Well-known psychopomps in the Old Norse Traditions are Odin, Freyja and the Valkyries. Psychopomps are often associated with animals such as horses, ravens, dogs, crows, owls, sparrows, harts, and dolphins.

ALGIZ – MADR = Animal Ancestors and Animal Allies The Shapeshifter and Theriantrope

Shamans often shape-shift into animals, to do spirit work. Travelling back through the Mists of Time, we find our Bacterial and Virus Ancestors here.

ALGIZ – LAGU = An Antlered Mother meets the Lady of the Lake

The Northern peoples were deer hunters and knew an Antlered Mother.

In the poem *Gylfaginning* (the deception of Gylfi) Norse god Freyr is forced to fight without any weapons against the giant Beli. Freyr eventually kills the giant with the antler of a stag.[102]

ALGIZ – ING = The Fertility of Wild Animals
This axis runs between the notorious fertility of rabbits and people with guns "controlling animal populations". It hosts many gnarly issues. Selective breeding of animals (for desirable qualities) leads to problems. Humans also control wildlife populations, paradoxically, to prevent the extinction of other species.

ALGIZ – ODAL = The Sovereignty of Animal Habitats and Territories
Loss of habitat and threats to their territories puts an ever-increasing number of animals at risk of extinction. The cure for this mindset involves re-wilding and *creating wild places of devotion to the land.*[103] And, in doing so we also rewild ourselves.

ALGIZ – DAGAZ = Antlered Enlightenment
On the winter solstice the Deer Mother carries the returning sun in her antlers. From myths and early stories we know that human beings and animals were once much closer; they shapeshifted into each other. By regaining (or reconnecting to) animal powers we regain vitality, a deeper respect for all beings and a deep respect for the life-death-rebirth cycle.

ALGIZ – FE = Rewilding
This axis invites us to put 'the feral' back in domesticated animals and to reclaim feral parts or ourselves. To step outside cultural and childhood conditioning and lead a wilder life, depending on what that means for you: *Less money or creature comforts but more freedom? Feeling fully alive again?*

SOL

This rune represents the physical sun – while Rune DAGAZ represents symbolic light: illumination and enlightenment.

SOL – TYR = The Solar Warrior

Here we meet the Solar Warrior, who fights many battles to bring light and peace to disturbed places and to human lives shattered by armed conflict.

SOL – BJARKA = The White Goddess or White Lady

Pay attention to the eerie white luminosity of the Birch Tree. Here we encounter the *Witte Wieven* from the pre-Christian folklore of the Low Countries. They are pale/white/wise ladies seen spinning on the Hunebedden (Passage Graves) in the east of the country. They were healers and had the gift of prophecy, which links them to the Norns.[104]

SOL – EH = Árvakr & Alsviðr

Árvakr means early riser (literally early awake) and *Alsviðr* means very fast or swift. They are the horses pulling the chariot of the Sun across the sky. *Skinfax*i and *Hrímfaxi* are the horses of Dagr (Day) and Nótt (Night).[105]

SOL – MADR = The Relationship Human Beings have with the Sun

On this axis we work on our (conflicted) relationship with the Sun. We depend on her light and heat for our very existence. We like sunbathing, but we don't like sunburn. We lather ourselves in suncream and worry about skin cancer. Lack of sunlight can lead to vitamin D deficiency, seasonal affective disorder, low energy and other health issues.

SOL – LAGU = The Blood Red Sun

The sun makes human existence on our planet possible and we speak of "life blood". The sun often turns red during sunrises or sunsets, an optical effect caused by atmospheric conditions.

SOL – ING

Sunshine and heat are required for seeds to sprout and grow into seedlings.

SOL – ODAL = The Home of the Sun & Our Solar Self

The paradox is that the sun has no home. She is forever circling the heavens, pursued by a wolf, her chariot pulled by two horses. In astrology the sun represents the self and is linked to willpower, ego and vitality.

SOL – DAGAZ = From Sunlight To Enlightenment

Rune SOL represents the (physical) Sun but Rune DAGAZ represents the light in every possible sense: spiritual, symbolic, metaphorical.

SOL – FE = The Cattle Of The Sun

In Greek mythology the god of the Sun, Helios, was described as having seven herds of oxen and seven flocks of sheep.[106] The (Finnish) Kalevala warns against molesting 'the Cattle of the Sun':

Never venture to approach thou//Where the golden herd is living.[107]

TYR

The Tyr rune is an arrow. I see it as pointing upward at the North Star (Polaris) and holding up the sky. Tyr is many things, and of them is a *planetary architect* or *architect of the cosmos*, the energetic structure supporting consciousness. He is also the spiritual warrior who sacrifices one hand (or arm).

TYR – BJARKA = Valkyrie and Shield Maiden
The Heroic Feminine
Female Sovereignty

This is the axis of the female warrior. Archaeologist Neil Price discovered that graves were often assumed to belong to male warriors but modern techniques, such as DNA testing, revealed some belong to female warriors.[108]

TYR – EH = The Axis of the Einherjar

The *Einherjar* are warriors who died on the battlefield and were led to Valhalla by Valkyries. The Einherjar are in daily training for fighting alongside Odin at Ragnarok.

TYR – MADR = The Career Soldier & the Scapegoat

Permanent armies consist of career soldiers who choose a military career (as opposed to a conscripted soldiers). This is also the axis of the scapegoat. Families, groups and communities often create scapegoats. It is a common (and unconscious) shadow-avoidance strategy ("outsourcing of blame").[109]

TYR – LAGU = The Return and Ritual Cleansing of the Warrior

Weapons of mass destruction have ruined the more positive qualities that war once fostered (rites of passage for young men, the mythical alignment with deities of war, the building of courage, the defence of loved ones and tribe etc.) Ancient societies had specific rites for welcoming their warriors home from battle and reintegrating them back into society.[110]

TYR – ING = Where a Warrior Plants the Seeds of Peace

As a teenager I would have voted blindly for the Netherlands dismantling their military forces overnight. At age 57 I know that War is a formidable cosmic force, deeply wired into the human soul. A person or country must be able to defend themselves. We need to manage the humanitarian dimension and prevent unnecessary suffering. Warriors (soldiers) also need to be trained in peacekeeping and human rights or else war will engulf them and make them traumatised "killing machines". As "the first on the scene", they need to plant "the seeds of peace".[111]

TYR – ODAL = The Lawspeaker at Assemblies

The word *Law Speaker* originates in a Germanic and Norse oral tradition, where wise people were asked to recite the law (because nothing was written down, gifted people committed all the laws to memory). Snorri Sturluson (1179 – 1241, author of the *Prose Edda*) was a Law Speaker in Iceland.

TYR – DAGAZ = Where the Spiritual Warrior Finds Enlightenment

They say that "all roads lead to Rome". The same thing is true for spirituality: there are many possible paths for evolving human consciousness and one is *the path of the warrior.*

TYR – FE = Spiritual Rewards

Soldiers plunder but spiritual warriors reap other rewards. People practicing an earth-based spirituality see divinity everywhere, even in all aspects of the physical world. The "rewards" include a deep connection to land, communication with ancestors and soul connections with kindred spirits.

BJARKA (BERKANA)

Birch tree and by extension the (Cosmic) Mother, rites of passage for women, apothecary, rune for healers.

BJARKA – EH = Rites and Traditions for the Dead Involving Birch

In Eastern Slavic funerary traditions, birch was used in preparations for a recently deceased person. Often a coffin was laid out with birch leaves and brooms. A pillow stuffed with birch leaves was placed under the head of the dead person. Sometimes a birch tree was planted on a grave.[112]

BJARKA – MADR = Ancestors Who Died Young Inhabiting Birch Trees

During Green Week (a Slavic festival celebrated in early June) the Ancestors, (especially those that died young) temporarily leave their "world" (home in the afterlife) and appear in the world of the living. In our world, they then inhabit birch trees.[113]

BJARKA – LAGU = Love Potions & Healing Elixirs

Slavic people made love potions from birch. A twig was left on a threshold that the "intended love object" would pass. Its leaves were pulverized and carried close to the heart of the lovesick person. They were secretly added to the love-object's drink.[114] This axis also describes the tides of sexual arousal:

BJARKA – ING = Pioneer Seeds

The seeds of birch trees are pioneers. Carried by the wind they travel great distances to open ground. Freyr represents seeds and growth, sap rising and new plants sprouting after winter, or on waste land, regeneration.

BJARKA – ING = The Cosmic Mother Carries All Seeds Within Her

A female foetus typically has around 6–7 million eggs at 20 weeks of gestation, dropping to 1–2 million at birth. The tiny egg that becomes (a large part) of us already existed long before we were born or conceived.[115]

BJARKA – ODAL = Maiden Sanctuary (in the past)
Safe Spaces for Women (in the 21st Century)

In the second half of the 20th century second-wave feminists campaigned for safe spaces for women, to reduce the risk of gender-based violence (statistically committed by men). In our day the category "woman" has been stretched to include men who self-identify as women. Not all women agree with cancelling all-women spaces.

BJARKA – DAGAZ = The Enlightened Mother

This is the axis of self-aware mothering and nourishing. Here healers do shadow work and tend to their own needs, so they can continue to be there for others.

BJARKA – FE = Abundantia (Mother Abundance)

In ancient Rome, Abundantia was a divine personification of abundance and prosperity. Norse goddess Sif comes closest to representing grain and abundance.

EH (EHWAZ)

Horse Rune and Rune of Death, rune of Partnership and Twins; excursions of the soul and mapping otherworld geography.

EH – MADR = Making Death Our Ally
DEATH DOULA WORK

Here we meet the Norse psychopomps: Odin, Freyja, the Valkyries and Modgudr (ON Móðguðr), who is the female guardian of the bridge over the river *Gjöll*. She allowed newly deceased people to cross this bridge and likely prevents the dead from returning. Separation between the living and the dead is essential for the well-being of all.

EH – LAGU = The Sea Steed
Where the Souls of the Dead Travel Over Water

Horse kennings are used in the Eddas to describe the sea. A kenning is a poetic circumlocution replacing an everyday word. Viking ships were "the horses of the sea" and their ships had carved animal heads.

EH – ING = The Axis of Alfheim (Freyr's Realm)

Here a transformation occurs, where male ancestors (so called Álfar or "Elves") become guardians of fertility and prosperity.

Note from my rune diary: *Grief is the fertile strip of land between Life and Death.*

EH – ODAL = The House of Death
Death was viewed as "contagious". The Sami avoided spots where a wolf or bear had devoured its pray, and the Estonians avoided places where human bones were found. In Sweden people avoided building houses in places "tainted by death".[116]

EH – DAGAZ = Death as the Ultimate Healing & Illumination
Some spiritual traditions teach that Death is the ultimate healing because we leave our vulnerable hurting body and return to the embrace of the Cosmic Mother or Ancestors.

EH – FE = Death Feeds Life
The harvest brings abundance courtesy of the scythe. Cows are milked and slaughtered. Death is intimately linked into food, abundance and wealth.

MADR

Rune of all matters related to human beings, including our ancestors and descendants.

MADR – LAGU = The Well of Ancestral Memory
Beyond our personal memory there is a reservoir of ancestral and collective memory. In Fennoscandia and Russia the sauna was also known as the House of the Ancestors (because births and deaths were tended to there).

MADR – ING = The Axis of Human Potential
The Personal Growth Mindset
This axis invites us to "become our best selves" and "have a growth mindset" (to use popular modern phrases). Human

potential is commonly defined as the innate ability of every person to live and perform in alignment with their highest self.

MADR – ODAL = Ancestral Home

In the past our ancestral land or property was also the place where our ancestors were buried. The Viking Age had no death penalty for heinous crimes. Instead, criminals were declared outlaws.[117]

MADR – DAGAZ = Enlightened Acts

This is the "axis of the Serenity Prayer": accept the things we cannot change but change things we can, and freeing ourselves from torment. Here we also find acts of courage, inspiration or redemption.

MADR – FE = Economics & Cattle Thieves

Economics has been defined as "the study of scarcity". Scarcity defines the value of things. This axis covers all aspects of fair distribution (fair wages, redistribution of wealth, funding to ensure care for vulnerable groups) and our personal relationship with money.

LAGU

Water in all its manifestations! By extension lunar tides, emotions, intuition, ability to go with the flow or be in flow.

LAGU – ING = Seedlings

Seeds and seedlings need regular watering. Symbolically speaking this axis invites us to reflect on the areas of our life we can rejuvenate by watering and tending more carefully. In a rune reading this axis might indicate fertility or pregnancy related issues.

LAGU – ODAL = Ancestral Blood and Sources of Water
The Hall of the Moon
Glitnir: Forseti's Golden Hall and Seat of Justice

This axis is the *Hall of the Moon* referenced in the *Poetic Edda.*[118] In Ancient Egypt the sacred lake next to the temple symbolised the primordial waters or Rivers of Nun. Here the priests bathed at dawn, before entering the temple.[119]

LAGU – DAGAZ = Liquid Light
The Philosopher's Stone

One of Freyja's names is Mardǫll, often translated as *light shining on water* and a kenning (poetic metaphor) for gold. This is the axis of liquid gold and liquid light. Alchemists toiled for years to turn base metals, such as lead, into gold but never produced the Philosopher's Stone.

LAGU – FE = To Liquidize
Milk as a Heavenly Elixir

Among the ancients, milk was regarded as heavenly nourishment and the elixir of regeneration. The Hindus still administer it to dying people.[120] Blenders and juicers have become popular kitchen gadgets while bankers speak of liquidizing assets.

ING

Seed, seedpod, storehouse of potential, rune of Freyr.

"Eros, to begin with, is not love between man and woman, but the impulse of life in all living things."[121]

ODAL – ING = Alfheimr

ODAL is derived from the Old Norse word *aðal*: the best part of a farm or land. In the Viking Age an Odal Farmer was someone whose family had lived on land for four generations. The Odal

Farmer and bloodline were considered connected to the land and he could not sell the property, as it did not belong to him personally, but to the entire bloodline. In modern Dutch this becomes the word "adel": meaning of noble birth, born into an aristocratic family.

ING – DAGAZ = Completion Of All That Seeks Form
Gestalt Psychology

This axis encapsulates the entire sequence from seed (or seed form or concept) to the completion of a cycle, and arrival at a higher perspective. Everything that takes form, seeks completion of its full (developmental or evolutionary) cycle.

ING – FE = From Seed To Abundance
The Reproductive Cycle

We see another completion of a cycle: from seed/semen and egg to fully-fledged cattle producing their own calves.

ODAL

House, family home, ancestral homestead.
By extension: temple, sacred enclosure, homeland.

The house is a microcosm of the world.[122]

At ODAL we build walls around our personal sanctuary, and we mark our boundary with a fence or a hedge. We make decisions about what is in and what stays out. The same thing happens on a larger level: countries have borders, passport-control and a foreign policy. Immigration is a red-hot topic at the time of writing this book.

ODAL – DAGAZ = Utopia or "Heaven on Earth"

This is the axis of an enlightened home and also of a spiritual school. On the ultimate level, it is our home in the other world, representing the continuation of consciousness after death.

Every human-made utopia sooner or later turns dystopian and the cycle of creation and destruction (a dialectic process) repeats itself.

ODAL – FE = House Prices
The Cost of Belonging
In a rune reading this axis might refer to house prices, a mortgage application, or deposit. It can also refer to the "cost of belonging": perhaps we a sacrifice a larger dream to live near our family? Operating outside of 'the rules of society or a family' (these structures are "ODALS" too) extracts a big price (scapegoating, being ostracized). In the Viking Age the minting of coins was well underway.

DAGAZ

Day, Light, enlightenment and illumination.
This is the rune of Norse god Dagr (Day).

DAGAZ – FE = SACRED KNOWLEDGE OF PRECESSION AND COSMIC CYCLES
DAGAZ is often described as a butterfly. When you tilt this rune by 90 degrees, you have an hourglass or analemma instead. In astronomy an analemma (which resembles a lemniscate, but one loop is smaller/shorter) is a diagram which shows the position of the sun in the sky, from one fixed location on Earth, always at the same solar time. Sunna's position shifts a little every day and a full year's worth of observations will give you a figure 8.[123]

FE

Cattle, wealth.

It could be argued that capitalism starts with domesticated cattle. At FE the wheel of the runes comes full circle but the wheel keeps turning. Next up is UR. There is a profoundly magical gap between FE and UR. I think of it as the *Ginnungagap*: the yawning void, or gaping abyss, filled with magical powers. Speaking on the cosmic level, Ragnarok occurs here: one cycle (or world) ends, and another cycle (or world) begins.

Endnotes

PART I

Preface

1. https://www.voluspa.org/havamal.htm
2. https://www.thecollector.com/what-is-plato-theory-of-forms/
3. *The Tradition of the Household Spirits: Ancestral Lore and Practices,* Inner Traditions, 2013 p. viii
4. *An Introduction to English Runes* by R.I. Page, The Boydell Press, 1999 reprint, p. 3
5. *An Introduction to English Runes* by R.I. Page, The Boydell Press, 1999 reprint, p. 16 - 21
6. https://www.gu.se/en/research/rok-runestone-revisited
7. https://www.vikingtimes.co.uk/viking-culture/viking-tattoos/

Chapter 1

1. https://www.hellinger.com/en/family-constellation/
2. https://numerologynation.com/numerology/
3. https://www.thedarkpixieastrology.com/blog/generational-astrology-in-the-natal-chart-decoding-family-secrets-by-planet-and-house-placement
4. *North Sea Water in my Veins (The Pre-Christian Spirituality of the Low Countries)* by Imelda Almqvist, 2022, Moon Books p. 295

Chapter 2

1. https://oldenglishpoetry.camden.rutgers.edu/the-rune-poem/
2. https://www.historyfiles.co.uk/FeaturesEurope/BarbarianTribes04.htm

Chapter 4

1. *Nightside of the Runes: Uthark, Adulruna, and the Gothic Cabbala* by Thomas Karlsson, Inner Traditions, 2019
2. https://norse-mythology.org/introduction-georges-dumezil/
3. https://www.medievalists.net/2016/01/those-who-pray-those-who-work-those-who-fight/

Chapter 5

1. https://www.omnicalculator.com/statistics/combination

Chapter 6

1. https://www.poetryintranslation.com/PITBR/Latin/PharsaliaImaster.php
2. *Myths of Greece and Rome,* by Jane Ellen Harrison, Zinc Read, 2023, p.4
3. *Myths of Greece and Rome,* by Jane Ellen Harrison, Zinc Read, 2023, p.4
4. *Myths of Greece and Rome,* by Jane Ellen Harrison, Zinc Read, 2023, p.9
5. *Myths of Greece and Rome,* by Jane Ellen Harrison, Zinc Read, 2023, p.8
6. http://www.egyptianmyths.net/bat.htm
7. https://henadology.wordpress.com/theology/netjeru/bat/
8. http://www.thewhitegoddess.co.uk/the_goddess/hathor_-_eye_of_ra.asp
9. *The Seed of Yggdrasill: Deciphering the Hidden Messages in Old Norse Myths,* by Maria Kvilhaug, Whyte Tracks, 2013, p. 89
10. http://www.3worlds.co.uk/Articles/Coat-of-Power.pdf
11. https://scfh.ru/en/papers/a-blacksmith-and-a-shaman/
12. https://modernnorseheathen.wordpress.com/2018/01/10/the-mystery-of-the-brisingamen/

13. *The Seed of Yggdrasill: Deciphering the Hidden Messages in Old Norse Myths,* by Maria Kvilhaug, Whyte Tracks, 2013, p.23
14. *Myths of Greece and Rome,* by Jane Ellen Harrison, Zinc Read, 2023, p.14
15. *The Seed of Yggdrasill: Deciphering the Hidden Messages in Old Norse Myths,* by Maria Kvilhaug, Whyte Tracks, 2013, p.71
16. https://open.substack.com/pub/imeldaalmqvist/p/today-the-crone-ties-the-cosmic-granny?r=2olbkh&utm_campaign=post&utm_medium=web&showWelcomeOnShare=false
17. https://www.science.org/content/article/relics-washed-beaches-reveal-lost-world-beneath-north-sea
18. https://www.edgemagazine.net/2014/12/winter-solstice-reindeer-goddess/
19. https://pantheon.org/articles/a/alfrodull.html
20. https://symbolsage.com/tyr-norse-god-of-war/
21. https://www.cambridge.org/core/journals/antiquity/article/viking-warrior-women-reassessing-birka-chamber-grave-bj581/7CC691F69FAE51DDE905D27E049FADCD
22. https://www.facebook.com/slavicmagpie
23. https://www.youtube.com/watch?v=2TaixdHbF-0
24. https://www.grottimill.com/en/prints/margygr-mermaid.php
25. https://www.therootdoctor.se/
26. https://imeldaalmqvist.substack.com/p/recruiting-a-house-spirit-essay-2?utm_source=publication-search

Chapter 7

1. https://fractalfoundation.org/resources/what-are-fractals/
2. https://www.thoughtco.com/what-is-quantum-entanglement-2699355

3. *Runic Astrology: Starcraft and Timekeeping in the Northern Tradition*, Aquarian Press; Reprint edition (12 July 1990)
4. *On the Origins of the Alphabet* by Brian R. Pellar, https://brianpellar.com/origins-of-alphabet
5. https://www.space.com/5417-ecliptic-zodiac-work.html
6. https://elemental-astrology.com/what-is-the-difference-between-zodiac-signs-and-houses-in-astrology/
7. *Northern Mysteries & Magick: Runes and Feminine Powers* by Freya Aswynn, Llewellyn Publications US, 2002, p. 139 - 141

Chapter 8

1. https://www.academia.edu/99832445/Alphabets_and_the_Mystery_Traditions
2. https://blog.prepscholar.com/greek-alphabet-letters-symbols
3. https://www.fathersalphabet.com/paleo-hebrew-alphabet-chart/
4. https://www.britannica.com/science/numeral/Development-of-modern-numerals-and-numeral-systems
5. https://www.gatewaystobabylon.com/myths/texts/classic/enmerkaratta.htm
6. https://www.cbc.ca/news/canada/newfoundland-labrador/hawthorn-hieroglyphs-alphabet-1.6288328
7. https://www.cbc.ca/news/canada/newfoundland-labrador/hawthorn-hieroglyphs-alphabet-1.6288328
8. http://www.angelfire.com/ks/larrycarter/Rowan/Tree.html
9. https://norse-mythology.org/gods-and-creatures/the-aesir-gods-and-goddesses/odin/
10. http://www.3worlds.co.uk/Articles/Coat-of-Power.pdf
11. https://academic.oup.com/book/25964/chapter-abstract/193771177?redirectedFrom=fulltext
12. https://journals.sagepub.com/doi/10.1177/2056305119872949
13. https://pantheon.org/articles/m/mundilfari.html

14. *The Norns in Old Norse Mythology* by Karen Bek-Pedersen, Dunedin Academic Press, 2013
15. https://www.britannica.com/science/cryonics
16. https://www.encyclopedia.com/environment/encyclopedias-almanacs-transcripts-and-maps/megalithic-religion-prehistoric-evidence
17. https://imeldaalmqvist.substack.com/p/the-twelve-days-of-christmas?utm_source=publication-search
18. https://www.britannica.com/topic/Leib-olmai
19. https://www.academia.edu/99832445/Alphabets_and_the_Mystery_Traditions
20. https://www.ancient-egypt-online.com/hieroglyphics-alphabet.html
21. https://vikingr.org/old-norse-texts/havamal
22. https://www.indo-european-connection.com/words/man
23. https://vikings-and-valhalla.com.au/blogs/rune-alphabet/laguz
24. https://earthandstarryheaven.com/2016/04/27/mimir-volsi/
25. https://www.sacredwicca.com/drawing-down-the-moon
26. https://plato.stanford.edu/entries/plato-timaeus/
27. https://lonerwolf.com/kundalini-awakening/
28. https://www.britannica.com/topic/Kali
29. https://www.learnreligions.com/kali-the-dark-mother-1770364

Chapter 9

1. https://www.norsemyth.org/2010/10/myth-science-thors-fishing-trip.html#:~:text=In%20Norse%20mythology,%20Thor%E2%80%99s%20mystic%20hammer%20is%20often,through%20the%20night%20sky,%20seemingly%20chasing%20the%20first.
2. https://www.csmonitor.com/Science/2011/0207/Did-Vikings-navigate-the-seas-using-crystals#:~:text=Research%20

shows%20that%20the%20Vikings%20may%20have%20navigated,Ship%20stands%20in%20front%20of%20Stockholm%27s%20National%20Museum.

3. https://www.skyatnightmagazine.com/advice/constellations-move-change-over-time
4. https://www.sanskritimagazine.com/the-hymn-of-creation-nasadiya-sukta/
5. https://mythsmysterieswonders.site/index.php/norse-constellations/
6. https://www.space.com/the-story-of-the-stars
7. https://www.mccookgazette.com/story/1720784.html
8. Faulkes translation, 1987:18-19
9. Elias Lönnrot 1989: 105
10. *Runic Astrology, Starcraft and Timekeeping in the Northern Tradition by Nigel Pennick*, p. 31-36
11. https://www.academia.edu/27629275/How_Passages_in_the_Edda_act_as_References_to_Constellations?auto=download&email_work_card=download-paper
12. Bellows Translation, 1923
13. http://aswynn.com/
14. https://sacred-texts.com/neu/poe/poe12.htm
15. https://www.academia.edu/27629275/How_Passages_in_the_Edda_act_as_References_to_Constellations?auto=download&email_work_card=download-paper
16. https://explainingscience.org/2020/09/25/the-changing-pole-star/
17. *The Arctic Sky: Inuit Astronomy, Starlore and Legend* by John MacDonald, 2000, Royal Ontario Museum
18. https://www.ancientpages.com/2017/12/16/horses-skinfaxi-hrimfaxi-bringers-light-darkness-earth-norse-mythology/
19. Vafþrúðnismál stanza 23
20. https://oldworldgods.com/norse/hjuki-and-bil/

21. https://www.renaissanceastrology.com/hermesfixedstars.html
22. *Pagan Magic of the Northern Tradition: Customs, Rites and Ceremonies* by Nigel Pennick, 2015, Destiny Books p. 181 – 196
23. https://www.deviantart.com/heathen-kindred/journal/Norse-Constellations-and-the-Astronomy-of-Myth-219759725
24. https://www.deviantart.com/heathen-kindred/journal/Norse-Constellations-and-the-Astronomy-of-Myth-219759725
25. https://www.deviantart.com/heathen-kindred/journal/Norse-Constellations-and-the-Astronomy-of-Myth-219759725
26. https://darkstarastrology.com/hyades/
27. https://norsemythologist.com/what-is-the-bifrost/
28. https://www.medievalists.net/2012/03/ancient-skies-of-northern-europe-stars-constellations-and-the-moon-in-nordic-mythology/
29. https://www.deviantart.com/heathen-kindred/journal/Norse-Constellations-and-the-Astronomy-of-Myth-219759725
30. https://www.britannica.com/biography/Saxo-Grammaticus
31. Faulkes 1987:18-19, https://1library.net/document/zwo87x1y-snorri-sturluson-edda-prologue-and-gylfaginning.html

Chapter 10

1. https://norse-mythology.org/concepts/the-parts-of-the-self/
2. *Wyrdwalkers: Techniques of Norther-Tradition Shamanism* by Raven Kaldera, Asphodel Press, 2006 p. 189 - 203
3. https://cleasby-vigfusson-dictionary.vercel.app/word/odr

4. https://kulturminnet.wordpress.com/2023/02/11/den-svenska-folktrons-ordlista-vasen-trolldom-skrock-och-sagner/
5. https://aswynn.com/category/blog/runes/
6. https://imeldaalmqvist.substack.com/p/sins-of-commission-and-omission
7. https://imeldaalmqvist.substack.com/p/prayer?utm_source=publication-search

Chapter 11

1. *Icelandic Magic: Practical Secrets of the Northern Grimoires* by Stephen E. Flowers, Inner Traditions, 2016
2. https://www.sagadb.org/egils_saga.en
3. http://ingridjonsson.com/trad-i-folktron/
4. https://www.youtube.com/watch?v=4a1CSgsJV5k
5. https://folkfiesta.net/en/post/askafroa-woman-ash-protects-trees/

Chapter 12

1. *Beyond the North Wind: The Fall and Rise of the Mystic North* by Christopher McIntosh, Red Wheel/Weiser, 2019, p.1
2. https://en.natmus.dk/historical-knowledge/denmark/prehistoric-period-until-1050-ad/the-viking-age/religion-magic-death-and-rituals/the-viking-blot-sacrifices/

PART II

1. *Witchcraft and Sorcery of the Balkans* by Radomir Ristic, Three Hands Press, 2015, p. 82 – 83
2. *Plants of the Devil* by Corinne Boyer, Three Hands Press, 2017, p. 29
3. *Outlandish: Walking Europe's Unlikely Landscapes* by Nick Hunt, 2021, John Murray, p. 91

4. *Plants of the Devil* by Corinne Boyer, Three Hands Press, 2017, p.8
5. *Courting the Wild Twin* by Martin Shaw, 2023, Chelsea Green Publishing UK
6. https://imeldaalmqvist.substack.com/p/spiritual-narcissism-part-2?utm_source=publication-search
7. *Woodruff's Guide to Slavic Deities* by Patricia Robin Woodruff, 2020, p.2
8. *Woodruff's Guide to Slavic Deities* by Patricia Robin Woodruff, 2020, p.11
9. https://www.vikingrune.com/2009/08/thors-hammer-norse-symbol/
10. *Plants of the Devil* by Corinne Boyer, Three Hands Press, 2017, p.29
11. https://www.britannica.com/topic/Yama-Hindu-god
12. *Plants of the Devil* by Corinne Boyer, Three Hands Press, 2017, p.31
13. https://www.shponline.co.uk/culture-and-behaviours/dealing-well-poisoners/
14. *Plants of the Devil* by Corinne Boyer, Three Hands Press, 2017, p.36
15. Mircea Eliade quoted in *The Tradition of Household Spirits: Ancestral Lore and Practices* by Claude Lecouteux, Inner Traditions, 2013, p. 26
16. *Witchcraft and Sorcery of the Balkans* by Radomir Ristic, Three Hands Press, 2015, p. 107
17. *Myths of Greece and Rome*, by Jane Ellen Harrison, Zinc Read, 2023, p. 68
18. *Outlandish: Walking Europe's Unlikely Landscapes* by Nick Hunt, 2021, John Murray, p. 125
19. *Outlandish: Walking Europe's Unlikely Landscapes* by Nick Hunt, 2021, John Murray, p. 126
20. *Myths of Greece and Rome*, by Jane Ellen Harrison, Zinc Read, 2023, p. 79

21. https://ausrineart.wordpress.com/tag/personalized-art/
22. https://rotergeysir.net/conversation-with-rudolf-simek/
23. https://sonsofvikings.com/blogs/history/history-of-viking-oath-rings
24. https://archive.org/details/MSNBCW_20131006_100000_Ted_Bundy_-_Death_Row_Tapes
25. *Myths of Greece and Rome*, by Jane Ellen Harrison, Zinc Read, 2023, p. 79
26. *Woodruff's Guide to Slavic Deities* by Patricia Robin Woodruff, 2020, p.3
27. *Woodruff's Guide to Slavic Deities* by Patricia Robin Woodruff, 2020, p. 252
28. *The Tradition of Household Spirits: Ancestral Lore and Practices* by Claude Lecouteux, Inner Traditions, 2013, p.8
29. *The Tradition of Household Spirits: Ancestral Lore and Practices* by Claude Lecouteux, Inner Traditions, 2013, p.4
30. *Woodruff's Guide to Slavic Deities* by Patricia Robin Woodruff, 2020, p.30
31. https://www.britannica.com/topic/Vainamoinen
32. *North Sea Water in My Veins: The Pre-Christian Spirituality of the Low Countries* by Imelda Almqvist, Moon Books, 2022, p. 178
33. *Witchcraft and Sorcery of the Balkans* by Radomir Ristic, Three Hands Press, 2015, p. 107
34. *Outlandish: Walking Europe's Unlikely Landscapes* by Nick Hunt, 2021, John Murray, p.60
35. https://www.arcus.org/witness-the-arctic/2016/2/article/25680#:~:text
36. *Woodruff's Guide to Slavic Deities* by Patricia Robin Woodruff, 2020, p.27
37. https://www.space.com/solar-flares-effects-classification-formation
38. https://bigthink.com/series/explain-it-like-im-smart/the-big-bang-gave-us-time/#:~:text=He%20explains%20that%20

the%20arrow%20of%20time%2C%20or,Universe%20began%20in%20a%20state%20of%20low%20entropy.
39. https://www.facebook.com/profile/100083157469761/search/?q=birch%20tree
40. https://www.voluspa.org/sigrdrifumal.htm
41. *North Sea Water in My Veins: The Pre-Christian Spirituality of the Low Countries* by Imelda Almqvist, Moon Books, 2022, p. 255
42. https://www.britannica.com/topic/Nerthus
43. https://www.thecharmworks.com/HistoryofCharms
44. *Witchcraft and Sorcery of the Balkans* by Radomir Ristic, Three Hands Press, 2015, p. 26 - 27
45. https://duversity.org/wp-content/uploads/2023/12/Methods-of-the-Soul2.pdf
46. https://folklorethursday.com/folklore-of-archaeology/ferrous-friend-foe-iron-became-enemy-fairy-folk/#:~:text=Some%20have%20suggested%20that%20this%20is%20where%20the,known%20as%20the%20enemy%20of%20the%20%E2%80%98fairy%20folk.%E2%80%99
47. https://www.britannica.com/topic/Saule
48. *Witchcraft and Sorcery of the Balkans* by Radomir Ristic, Three Hands Press, 2015, p. 26 - 27
49. https://www.azquotes.com/author/22090-Marion_Woodman
50. *King Arthur and the Goddess of the Land: the Divine Feminine in the Mabinogion* by Caitlin Matthews, Inner Traditions Bear and Company, 2002
51. https://artsofthought.com/2020/05/30/carl-jung-synchronicity/
52. https://dictionary.cambridge.org/dictionary/english/serendipity
53. *Myths of Greece and Rome,* by Jane Ellen Harrison, Zinc Read, 2023, p. 30
54. https://happymag.tv/animals-we-thought-were-extinct-but-actually-arent/

55. https://www.arborday.org/trees/treefacts/#:~:text=Trees%20provide%20us%20with%20oxygen.%201%20One%20large,in%20the%20Amazon%20Rainforest%20share%20Rain%20Forest%20Alliance
56. https://www.youtube.com/watch?v=yY7AdwI-r5Y
57. https://en.natmus.dk/historical-knowledge/denmark/prehistoric-period-until-1050-ad/the-viking-age/religion-magic-death-and-rituals/the-viking-blot-sacrifices/
58. https://norsemythologist.com/norse-runes-for-protection
59. Årsskrift-2014-s-32-40-Christian-Valeur-Björken-älskad-hatad-och-älskad-igen.pdf (skogshistoria.se)
60. *Witchcraft and Sorcery of the Balkans* by Radomir Ristic, Three Hands Press, 2015, p. 20 - 21
61. https://www.youtube.com/watch?v=HxFgL-rhgIw&feature=youtu.be&fbclid=IwAR0JSri0u-TJ-tUJb-KY7W_xPF0agPQpmKb0kFXTgUx-8dqiDEd1g7zHBeEU
62. *The Tradition of Household Spirits: Ancestral Lore and Practices* by Claude Lecouteux, Inner Traditions, 2013, p.15
63. https://www.brainyquote.com/topics/joy-quotes_2
64. https://imeldaalmqvist.substack.com/p/the-scapegoat?r=2olbkh
65. https://www.brainyquote.com/topics/joy-quotes_7
66. https://www.brainyquote.com/topics/joy-quotes
67. https://imeldaalmqvist.substack.com/p/longevity?utm_source=publication-search
68. https://palacegatecounsellingservice.wordpress.com/2018/12/06/francis-weller-on-grief/
69. https://seohelrune.com/2020/09/16/heathen-deity-relationships/
70. *Woodruff's Guide to Slavic Deities* by Patricia Robin Woodruff, 2020, p.9
71. *Plants of the Devil* by Corinne Boyer, Three Hands Press, 2017, p.82

72. *Plants of the Devil* by Corinne Boyer, Three Hands Press, 2017, p.79
73. *Outlandish: Walking Europe's Unlikely Landscapes* by Nick Hunt, 2021, John Murray, p.16
74. *Witchcraft and Sorcery of the Balkans* by Radomir Ristic, Three Hands Press, 2015, p.94 – 95
75. *Witchcraft and Sorcery of the Balkans* by Radomir Ristic, Three Hands Press, 2015, p. 144 - 145
76. https://www.ancientpages.com/2017/12/21/elli-norse-goddess-and-symbol-of-old-age-that-no-one-ever-could-defeat/
77. *Witchcraft and Sorcery of the Balkans* by Radomir Ristic, Three Hands Press, 2015, p. 28
78. https://www.ragweedforge.com/rpie.html
79. https://ausrineart.wordpress.com/tag/personalized-art/
80. https://www.facebook.com/ladyofthe.labyrinth/posts/the-nine-worlds-of-norse-mythology-fact-or-fictionevery-once-in-a-while-i-encoun/1634929269876286/
81. https://ausrineart.wordpress.com/tag/personalized-art/
82. https://www.worldhistory.org/Bronze_Age_Collapse/
83. *Plants of the Devil* by Corinne Boyer, Three Hands Press, 2017, p.51
84. https://anotherrhythm.wordpress.com/2014/12/27/the-wild-hunt-werewolves-and-divination-rauhnachte-in-europe/
85. *The Krampus and the Old, Dark Christmas: Roots and Rebirth of the Folkloric Devil* by Al Ridenour, Feral House, 2016, p. 136
86. https://namforsen.com/english/
87. https://vikingr.org/old-norse-texts/hymiskvida
88. https://www.facebook.com/authormaria.kvilhaug
89. *Witchcraft and Sorcery of the Balkans* by Radomir Ristic, Three Hands Press, 2015, p. 140

90. https://www.artandpopularculture.com/Womb_tomb
91. https://thewillowweb.com/2016/11/25/deer-folklore-faerie-cattle-sacred-sika-and-our-wild-sides/
92. *Plants of the Devil* by Corinne Boyer, Three Hands Press, 2017, p.24
93. *Outlandish: Walking Europe's Unlikely Landscapes* by Nick Hunt, 2021, John Murray, p.105
94. *Outlandish: Walking Europe's Unlikely Landscapes* by Nick Hunt, 2021, John Murray, p.76
95. *North Sea Water in My Veins: The Pre-Christian Spirituality of the Low Countries* by Imelda Almqvist, Moon Books, 2022, p.7
96. *Witchcraft and Sorcery of the Balkans* by Radomir Ristic, Three Hands Press, 2015, p. 149
97. *Outlandish: Walking Europe's Unlikely Landscapes* by Nick Hunt, 2021, John Murray, p.75
98. *The Tradition of Household Spirits: Ancestral Lore and Practices* by Claude Lecouteux, Inner Traditions, 2013, p.23
99. *The Tradition of Household Spirits: Ancestral Lore and Practices* by Claude Lecouteux, Inner Traditions, 2013, p.25
100. https://www.verywellmind.com/life-and-death-instincts-2795847
101. *Outlandish: Walking Europe's Unlikely Landscapes* by Nick Hunt, 2021, John Murray, p.41
102. https://link.springer.com/chapter/10.1007/978-3-031-37503-3_2
103. *Plants of the Devil* by Corinne Boyer, Three Hands Press, 2017, p.24
104. *North Sea Water in My Veins: The Pre-Christian Spirituality of the Low Countries* by Imelda Almqvist, Moon Books, 2022, p.152
105. https://pantheon.org/articles/a/arvakr_and_alsvidr.html
106. https://www.greekmyths-interpretation.com/en/odysseus-charybdis-interpretation/
107. https://sacred-texts.com/neu/kveng/kvrune49.htm

108. https://www.cambridge.org/core/journals/antiquity/article/viking-warrior-women-reassessing-birka-chamber-grave-bj581/7CC691F69FAE51DDE905D27E049FADCD
109. https://imeldaalmqvist.substack.com/p/the-scapegoat
110. *War and the Soul: Healing Our Nation's Veterans from Post-Traumatic Stress Disorder* by Edward Tick, Quest Books, 2005, p. 184 - 185
111. https://www.undp.org/blog/planting-seeds-peace-breaking-cycles-crisis
112. https://www.facebook.com/slavicmagpie
113. https://www.facebook.com/slavicmagpie
114. https://www.facebook.com/slavicmagpie
115. https://www.naturalcycles.com/cyclematters/5-facts-about-the-female-egg-cell
116. *By the Fire: Sami Folktales and Legends, collected and illustrated* by Emilie Demant Hatt, translated by Barbara Sjöholm, University of Minnesota Press, p.36
117. https://norse-mythology.org/outlawry-viking-age/
118. https://gcelt.org/the-enchanting-world-of-norse-words-for-stars-unveiling-the-vikings-celestial-language/
119. https://www.ancientpages.com/2018/04/05/daily-life-of-priests-and-priestesses-in-ancient-egypt/
120. https://www.myfarewelling.com/article/hindu-funeral
121. *Myths of Greece and Rome*, by Jane Ellen Harrison, Zinc Read, 2023, p.81
122. Ronald Grambo in his Foreword for *The Tradition of Household Spirits: Ancestral Lore and Practices* by Claude Lecouteux, Inner Traditions, 2013, p. ix
123. https://lovethenightsky.com/what-is-an-analemma/

Recommended Reading

Books

An Introduction to English Runes by R. I. Page, The Boydell Press, 1999 reprint

Nightside of the Runes: Uthark, Adulruna and Gothic Cabbala by Thomas Karlsson, Inner Traditions, 2019

Northern Mysteries & Magick: Runes and Feminine Powers by Freya Aswynn, Llewellyn Publications US, 2022

Alphabets and the Mystery Traditions: The Origins of Letters in the Earth, the Underworld, and the Heavens by Judith Dillon, Inner Traditions, 2024

The Seed of Yggdrasill: Deciphering the Hidden Messages in Old Norse Myths, by Maria Kvilhaug, Whyte Tracks, 2013

Runes and Astrology: Symbol and Starcraft in the Northern Tradition by Nigel Pennick, Destiny Books, 2023

Trolldom: Spells and Methods of the Norsk Folk Magic Tradition by Johannes Björn Gårdbäck, Yippie, 2015

Icelandic Magic: Practical Secrets of the Northern Grimoires by Stephen E. Flowers, Inner Traditions, 2016

Wyrdwalkers: Techniques of Northern-Tradition Shamanism by Raven Kaldera, Asphodel Press, 2006 p. 189 – 203

The Norns in Old Norse Mythology by Karen Bek-Pedersen, Dunedin Academic Press, 2013

Pagan Magic of the Northern Tradition: Customs, Rites and Ceremonies by Nigel Pennick, Destiny Books, 2015

Beyond the North Wind: The Fall and Rise of the Mystic North by Christopher McIntosh, Red Wheel/Weiser, 2019

Dictionary of Northern Mythology by Rudolph Simek and Angela Hall, D.S. Brewer, 1996

Witchcraft and Sorcery of the Balkans by Radomir Ristic, Three Hands Press, 2015

The Tradition of Household Spirits: Ancestral Lore and Practices by Claude Lecouteux, Inner Traditions, 2013

Woodruff's Guide to Slavic Deities by Patricia Robin Woodruff, 2020

Plants of the Devil by Corinne Boyer, Three Hands Press, 2017

The Krampus and the Old, Dark Christmas: Roots and Rebirth of the Folkloric Devil by Al Ridenour, Feral House, 2016

Myths of Greece and Rome, by Jane Ellen Harrison, Zinc Read, 2023

Outlandish: Walking Europe's Unlikely Landscapes by Nick Hunt, John Murray, 2021

The Arctic Sky: Inuit Astronomy, Starlore and Legends, by John MacDonald, Royal Ontario Museum, 2000

Courting the Wild Twin by Martin Shaw, 2023, Chelsea Green Publishing UK, 2023

War and the Soul: Healing Our Nation's Veterans from Post-Traumatic Stress Disorder by Edward Tick, Quest Books, 2005

By the Fire: Sami Folktales and Legends, collected and illustrated by Emilie Demant Hatt, translated by Barbara Sjöholm, University of Minnesota Press, 2019

Please note that my previous book contains a guide to the Frisian Runes:

North Sea Water in My Veins: The Pre-Christian Spirituality of the Low Countries by Imelda Almqvist, Moon Books, 2022

PDF's (Free downloads)

On the Origins of the Alphabet by Brian R. Pellar: free download from https://brianpellar.com/origins-of-alphabet

A Systematic Re-evaluation of the Sources of Old Norse Astronomy by Christian Etheridge, *read the full PDF online at:* https://www.cultureandcosmos.org/pdfs/16/Etheridge_INSAPVII_Old_Norse_Astronomy.pdf

How Passages in the Edda act as References to Constellations by Chris Johnsen https://www.academia.edu/27629275/How_Passages_in_the_Edda_act_as_References_to_Constellations?auto=download&email_work_card=download-paper

Coat of Power, a free article from Sacred Hoop Magazine: http://www.3worlds.co.uk/Articles/Coat-of-Power.pdf

Other useful sources

MagPie's Corner – East Slavic Rituals, Witchcraft and Culture (Facebook Community) https://www.facebook.com/slavicmagpie

I post regular essays (on a variety of topics, including runes and Old Norse traditions) on my Substack: https://imeldaalmqvist.substack.com/

The Stellarium App, (free download), software planetarium (sky maps from different cultures) https://stellarium-web.org/

MOON BOOKS

PAGANISM & SHAMANISM

What is Paganism? A religion, a spirituality, an alternative belief system, nature worship? You can find support for all these definitions (and many more) in dictionaries, encyclopaedias, and text books of religion, but subscribe to any one and the truth will evade you. Above all Paganism is a creative pursuit, an encounter with reality, an exploration of meaning and an expression of the soul. Druids, Heathens, Wiccans and others, all contribute their insights and literary riches to the Pagan tradition. Moon Books invites you to begin or to deepen your own encounter, right here, right now. If you have enjoyed this book, why not tell other readers by posting a review on your preferred book site.

Bestsellers from Moon Books

Keeping Her Keys

An Introduction to Hekate's Modern Witchcraft

Cyndi Brannen

Blending Hekate, witchcraft and personal development together to create

a powerful new magickal perspective.

Paperback: 978-1-78904-075-3 ebook 978-1-78904-076-0

Journey to the Dark Goddess

How to Return to Your Soul

Jane Meredith

Discover the powerful secrets of the Dark Goddess and transform your depression, grief and pain into healing and integration.

Paperback: 978-1-84694-677-6 ebook: 978-1-78099-223-5

Shamanic Reiki

Expanded Ways of Working with Universal Life Force Energy

Llyn Roberts, Robert Levy

Shamanism and Reiki are each powerful ways of healing; together, their power multiplies. Shamanic Reiki introduces techniques to help healers and Reiki practitioners tap ancient healing wisdom.

Paperback: 978-1-84694-037-8 ebook: 978-1-84694-650-9

Southern Cunning

Folkloric Witchcraft in the American South

Aaron Oberon

Modern witchcraft with a Southern flair, this book is a journey through the folklore of the American South and a look at the power these stories hold for modern witches.

Paperback: 978-1-78904-196-5 ebook: 978-1-78904-197-2

Bestsellers from Moon Books
Pagan Portals Series

The Morrigan

Meeting the Great Queens

Morgan Daimler

Ancient and enigmatic, the Morrigan reaches out to us. On shadowed wings and in raven's call, meet the ancient Irish goddess of war, battle, prophecy, death, sovereignty, and magic.

Paperback: 978-1-78279-833-0 ebook: 978-1-78279-834-7

The Awen Alone

Walking the Path of the Solitary Druid

Joanna van der Hoeven

An introductory guide for the solitary Druid, The Awen Alone will accompany you as you explore, and seek out your own place within the natural world.

Paperback: 978-1-78279-547-6 ebook: 978-1-78279-546-9

Moon Magic

Rachel Patterson

An introduction to working with the phases of the Moon, what they are and how to live in harmony with the lunar year and to utilise all the magical powers it provides.

Paperback: 978-1-78279-281-9 ebook: 978-1-78279-282-6

Hekate

A Devotional

Vivienne Moss

Hekate, Queen of Witches and the Shadow-Lands, haunts the pages of this devotional bringing magic and enchantment into your lives.

Paperback: 978-1-78535-161-7 ebook: 978-1-78535-162-4

Readers of ebooks can buy or view any of these bestsellers by clicking on the live link in the title. Most titles are published in paperback and as an ebook. Paperbacks are available in traditional bookshops. Both print and ebook formats are available online.

For video content, author interviews and more, please subscribe to our YouTube channel.

MoonBooksPublishing

Follow us on social media for book news, promotions and more:

Facebook: Moon Books

Instagram: @MoonBooksCI

Blog: https://thepagancollective.com

TikTok: @MoonBooksCI